ARTHUR RICHTER

DISTASTEFUL INTENT

Copyright @2021 by Arthur Richter

All rights reserved. No part of this book may be reproduced in any form or by any electronic or mechanical means, including information storage and retrieval systems, without permission in writing from the publisher, except by reviewers, who may quote brief passages in a review.

This publication contains the opinions and ideas of its author. It is intended to provide helpful and informative material on the subjects addressed in the publication. The author and publisher specifically disclaim all responsibility for any liability, loss or risk, personal or otherwise, which is incurred as a consequence, directly or indirectly, of the use and application of any of the contents of this book.

WORKBOOK PRESS LLC
187 E Warm Springs Rd,
Suite B285, Las Vegas, NV 89119, USA

Website:	https://workbookpress.com/
Hotline:	1-888-818-4856
Email:	admin@workbookpress.com

Ordering Information:
Quantity sales. Special discounts are available on quantity purchases by corporations, associations, and others.
For details, contact the publisher at the address above.

ISBN-13:	978-1-955459-41-9 (Paperback Version)
	978-1-955459-42-6 (Digital Version)

REV. DATE: 19/05/2021

ARTHUR RICHTER

CHAPTER 1

The year was 1962, the Place Milwaukee Wisconsin. My mother's was name was Helen Jones. She was only seventeen, years old, who eventually had to drop out of high school to take care of the house, and her three younger brothers while my mother worked.

Having no social life of her own who was feeling abused, taken for granted, and deprived and decided that she was going too runaway and create a new life for herself. Since she was nine, years old when her father died from leukemia.

Who after spending over a week with her best friend Betty from school Betty took her to cordially meet one of her friends. Where she meets for the first time Thomas Smith at his apartment.

Helen never had a life to speak of until the time she run away from home. Where Betty managed convince to Helen that it wasn't safe to stay at her place anymore, and told her that she knew of this very close friend of hers who she knows would help her find a place for herself, and could even take care of her as a favor to her.

Until her mother stopped coming to her house asking about her. Telling Helen that if she wasn't sure she would be safe with her friend she wouldn't think of taking her to meet him.

Thomas was twenty-two, at the time, and to say the least, handsome as all get out. Betty as well as a lot of other young girls got to knew Thomas very well through Betty after Betty got to know about him through her older brother.

Who was a close friend of his, and the two of them got to know each other, but because of her age he never took a personal interest in her in any other way, but as a friend even though she was extremely attractive and might had hesitated if she was over eighteen.

It was mostly through Betty's brother Bill that Tom got to find out a lot more than her wanted to about his sister Betty but as long as she kept her life to herself he considered her as a friend.

Where unbeknown to Helen when she walked into his apartment. That it would take him less than a day to add her to his list of conquests of young admirers. Where if she did she never would have agreed to go with Betty to his place.

At the age of seventeen, Helen was nothing less than a sensational looking redhead, with gorgeous blue eyes.

All of Helen's splendor was configured within a body of a 5 foot, 6 inches, tall red-haired bombshell. That all but defined her as the glamorous reincarnation of Marion Monroe herself not weighing more than 95 pounds soaking wet.

The second she walked in with her friend Betty, Helen's sinuousness attracted Tom's attention immediately.

Even though Tom was twenty-two, and Helen was only seventeen, looking twenty, he knew that it was going to be extremely difficult to avoid her, and Tom was not one to take risky chances. Knowing the life style he was leading.

The second Helen laid her eyes on him she became alarmingly intimated and fearful more of herself than of him.

* * * *

I came remember the way my mother described him as if she told me for the first time. As if knowing that her life was just now beginning, as well as over from wanting anything else but him out of her life.

Where she eventually found herself standing before the justice of the peace getting married against her mother's wishes. To the man of her dreams, Thomas Smith.

"Saying to me. I'll never forget the second my heart stopped and I found myself speechless not knowing how to describe Thomas other than to give my own prospective as to what his appearance was like.

He was nothing less than extremely charming, and extravagantly debonair far exceeding the way Betty described him, but as one who could have any women he laid his eyes on. "

Then mystically went on to describe his features in detail. Saying that he stood over 6-foot-tall, and couldn't have weight more than around 180 pounds.

Slim around the waist with a muscular physique from the shoulders down, extremely athletic looking, with facial features being physically masculine, and even more so desirable with those sparkling blues eyes looking into here's, and with his ungroomed light brown hair just brushed to one side making him look mysteriously devilish.

"My first thought the second I became enchanted with his captivating charm was. "On wonder why any women would do anything he ask her too… They would do it just from out of wanting to be his pride and joy. "

Then she went on telling me what Betty told her that she found out about him that she was finding very difficult to believe until she first laid her eyes on him and startlingly believed every word she said about him. Then going on to elaborate on about what she then discovered about him.

Saying that he was also a sergeant in the special forces who severed his country in an elite unit called the Derby Rangers, who was also well highly trained in the Martial Arts. Who was also believed to be involved with working for the syndicate.

Where Betty enthusiastically attempted to even make him sound even all that much more desirably exciting to get to know.

It wasn't until later on in my life that my mother finally confirmed what Betty told her about him actually working for the syndicate.

Telling me that she didn't come to find out about his syndicate connections until she started to meet some of his friends that he associated with on a regular basis later on.

That's when she discovers that he was what was known as a collector.

Who's source of income was attached to working as a bouncer which was a front to cover up who he was really working for, and what he was doing, when he was supposed to be working at a place called the Tike Club.

That was a topless Go-Go bar ran by a very sinuous madam who would do anything for him from out of admiration, and love for him.

Then only to discover that when she first met Tom. The police were involved in investigating him because that they wanted to put him behind bars really bad.

Mainly because they could never catch him at anything, and he did a hell of a lot of breaking the law and was getting away with it.

* * * *

Even though, my mother knew actually nothing about Tom other than what Betty said about him when Betty first took her to his apartment.

She was still relying heavily in Betty's judgement and trusted in her guaranteeing that she had nothing to be concerned about him, and that he was an alright guy, and only wanted to help her out. She never contemplated in her instantly becoming instantly spellbound at first sight of him.

Skeptical as she was about meeting him, and the fact that she was feeling very uncomfortable about meeting him.

She went along to go meet him under the understanding that if she didn't feel comfortable Betty would find some excuse for them both to leave.

What Helen didn't know was Betty had every intention of dumping Helen on him so that she could finally get rid of her, and didn't want to have the responsibility of having her around and having to hide her.

Seeing that she was under age and she didn't want to get caught contributing to a minor. Seeing that she was into doing her own thing on the streets, and didn't want her out competing against her.

The way Tom overcame her first impression of him was by overcoming what he thought was her skepticism him, and made her feel at ease.

By praying on her ignorance, and aliveness paying special attention her so that she might become sort of infatuated by him.

Applying congenial mannerisms when he first greeted her, and presented himself when he was introduced her when he welcomed her into his apartment, smilingly welcoming her into his apartment.

Readily accepting what Betty was telling him about her as he smiled cordially not asking a lot of personal questions about herself, just accepting her warmly into his home, keeping his distance from her, and not making her feel apprehensive about him harboring any desirable intention, by not dwelling on her appearance, or attractiveness.

Tom was a manipulator that Helen wasn't mentally prepared to encounter and his charming mannerism and his cordial demeanor put her at ease over any fear she might have concerning her physical welfare.

What she didn't anticipate was Betty deserting her by ling to her. Telling her that she had to leave, but she was going to be coming back after she took care of something, and convincing her that she had nothing to worry about when Tom was concern.

By taking Helen aside telling her that Tom was already involved with his girlfriend, and he could be trusted.

After Betty left Tom conducted himself like a true gentleman. They talked, watched TV, he even ordered a pizza as they listen to music on the radio after the TV went off the air for the night.

It wasn't until around midnight that I started to feel uneasy tired. Where he sorts of took notice that I was feeling uncomfortable about what was going to happen next, and was getting very nervous about Betty not showing up like she promised too.

I didn't want to tell him that she was a runaway and that she was only 17, going on 18, but there was no way she was going to leave, and find herself on the streets alone in the middle of the night.

Tom couldn't help but to notice that Helen was struggling to stay awake, and it became apparently obvious to him that Betty wasn't coming back, and that she obviously dumped her off at his place to get rid of her.

Tom knew Betty for the bitch that she was, and he couldn't see tossing Helen out onto the streets so he offered her to spend the night.

Offering her to let her sleep in his bedroom. Saying that it had a locking door, and she could lock it if I wasn't feeling safe.

I couldn't keep my eyes open so I took the chance, and accepted his offer, and went into his bedroom, locking the door behind me.

Once inside and all alone my curiosity got the better of me, so much so I inquisitively started looking through his closet and dresser drawers.

I was astonished at first too see an assortment of women clothing hanging on hangers in the closet and in the dresser drawers that I was looking into.

Then it dawned on me about what Betty said about him going with some women, and then it started to make sense as to why she was finding what she was finding which inspired her to even become involved snooping though things.

When he startlingly knocked on the door asking. If I was still awake and feeling alright, and if he come in.

I was stilled dressed, and already finished rifling through the dresser drawer and was in the process of closing it already and stood thinking to myself.' That it was his room.' So I let him in. Not realizing that I left the dresser drawer ajar.

Spotting it. I panicky pretended not to notice leaning against it. Nervously not knowing what he might do if he caught me snooping around in his things.

"Relax Helen." He calmly spoke out saying." You're welcome to anything you want. I can't wear them. They belonged to my ex-girlfriend. There's nothing for you to get upset about. No one is going to hurt you here. I know what it's like to be all alone, and frighten I've been there myself."

He was right. For the first time in my life I really was frighten not only for being totally overwhelmed and feel emotionally unstable even being close to him.

Along with the haunting hear over never being alone with a grown man before that I knew nothing at all about.

All sorts of horrid thoughts ran ramped through my mind about being raped, killed or worse unimaginable things befalling me.

I just couldn't handle the stress any longer. I broke down emotionally crying burying my face in my hands standing before him totally at his mercy to do whatever he wanted to too me.

When he walked up to me, and took me in his strong comforting arms hugging me. Letting me cry my eyes dry.

Just holding me not saying a words just consoling me until I felt comfortable being held in his arms against him.

His strong muscular arms felt so consoling... Like my father's arms use to feel when he holds me in his arms. They always made me feel safe and secure.

Tom's compassionate mature assured me that I had nothing to fear. His sensitivity, and consoling warmth caused me to close my swollen eyelids.

Emotionally feeling dizzy and physically weak where I was having trouble standing, and the more comforted I became the more submissively I relied on him to keep me safe.

I wrapped my arms around his waist and held onto him. Finding myself dependent on him not to let him go no longer harboring any fear of falling, as I drifted further and further into nothingness a slumber off inside his retaining arms.

* * * *

Where I startlingly woke. Panicky jerked up from utter fright. Panicky feeling about myself to find myself still in my clothes.

Thinking horrifying thoughts about what he could have done to me, but not a single button was unbuttoned, and I was still wearing my bra and panties.

Inquisitively I ventured to pull up my dress to feel between my legs examining myself. Concentrating on my pelvic region and my underpants.

Feeling for anything strange or any uncomfortable sensations that could indicate that I had been abused sexually.

Feeling nothing out of the ordinary until I knew for sure that my virginity was still in tacked. Still feeling totally petrified over the fact that I place myself in such a venerable position with him.

Nervously looking towards the door seeing it closed, and him nowhere in sight too propose a threat to my welfare. Gasping out a relieving sighing breath of relief over being intact and unarmed.

Cover myself back up with my shirt not daring to take my eyes of the closed door, not wanting him to come in catching me by surprise exposing myself and that I was examining myself maybe putting him on the defensive thinking that I wasn't trusting him.

Then rouse up to sit on the edge of the bed, and looked at the clock on the night stand reading 2:30. Then rouse from the bed and went to peer out door into the living room.

To see him still awake sitting on the sofa in his underwear, drinking a drink and reading the newspaper.

When he looked up and caught me staring at him. He immediately covered himself up saying." Well, what woke you up…?"

"I don't know…" I replied walking out of the bedroom into the living room to sit down beside him on the sofa, sorrowfully speaking out to him.

"I'm sorry if I'm such a burden on you, but I'm so confused… What am I going to do…?" I once again started to become emotionally distraught, struggling to hold back my tears of regret over doing something so stupid as to go running away from home.

"You mustn't concern yourself about that right now." He replied answering me as if known what I was so upset about. We all go through it at first. I myself even had to go through it even though I was a lot younger than you're right now.

Believe me when I say. "You will manage just like everyone else found themselves doing. Running away from home took a lot of courage to do for me, and I'm sure it was even harder for yourself to do you being a young attractive girl.

Especially at night when the world appears a lot more ominously threatening, and being in amongst strangers who could care less about what's going on in your life, or who are only looking for a change to pray on you. If you dared to let them know just how frighten you really are.

I was ten, when I ran away so there's nothing you could be feeling right now that I don't know how horrifically traumatic being alone and accentually by yourself.

I didn't want to address this but I knew the second Betty left that she wasn't coming back and it didn't take much for me to figure out that she dumped you off on me and that you were a runaway.

I've known Betty for some time now her brother is a close friend of mind. I don't want to diminish your choice of friends but, Betty can be a real bitch when she wants to be, and that's I feel justified to say about her right now.

You're welcome to make this your home for as long as you want, but you mustn't do anything hastily. I learnt right off to take a second to think about what you're doing and not acting impulsively.

So might I strongly suggest that you always think before you do anything. Regardless the pressure you might be under, and when you do. Trust your instincts and react accordingly. Think not of doing it, but what it will take to do it, and how it will affect you personally.

Helen I'm not going to say that you got lucky that Betty brought you to me. You could have wound up like so many other runaways do.

Finding themselves on the streets, sleeping in gutters, or being sold too guys by some pimp, or being raped, and left in some dark revolting alley, or doing gross disguising thing for something to eat.

It's a nasty cruel world out there. Where no one cares about anyone but themselves. Never forget that, and never trust in anyone, but yourself, and your instincts.

They will never lie and remember this. Your best friend is your worst enemy. So never say anything more than you have to about yourself to anyone that can be used against you, or could make you any more special than anyone else. You must blend in, and not stand out too draw attention to yourself."

"Why should you be any different than anyone else?"

"I'm not. I just don't have anything to gain for taking advantage of you. You're a young naive girl who needs a chance to be herself. I'm willing to give you that chance as long as you don't attempt to abuse it, or to betray my trust

All I ask is that what you see, hear, or bear witness to doesn't go beyond here to anyone else while you're here, and after you leave. This place never existed. Do you agree?"

"Yes, but that still doesn't help me with my problem."

"What problem? I don't see you having any problems. You've a place to sleep, food to eat, and clothes to wear. As for money, and a job maybe I could help you there as well."

"But what will I've to do for it?"

"Well, you could clean, cook, and wash the clothes, and dishes. I can hire you as a live in maid at minimum wage of course. You do know how to cook don't you?"

"Sure I do."

"Well do you want the job, or don't you? I'm out most nights. I work as a bouncer, and sometimes I'm gone for a few days.

As far as you're concern you'll be pretty much on your own, but if anyone should ask. I was home sleeping. Now that's your most important obligation to me.

I mean anyone, and that even includes the police. Especially the police, the police and I don't get along so good, and when I'm not home, if someone should knock on the door never answer it unless I'm here with you."

"But what if the police should come here and catch me?"

"They won't catch you if you don't tell them who you're. Never give your last name, but if by chance you should forget and they do.

Give them whatever name you want, and say you're only the part-time maid I hired, and lie about your age. You could pass for twenty, easy.

As for clothes my ex-girlfriend was about your size. They should suffice for the time being. Now as for the neighbors.

You're my sister, and don't mingle with the neighbors. As for boyfriend's no one come in this apartment but me. Do you understand…? I'm going to be very strict on that point."

"What about you? I mean I'll be living here with you…?"

"Don't concern yourself. As beautiful as you're. You're too young I've this golden rule I live by, and you don't fall into any of the categories."

"What about Betty? She's as young as I am, and she seems to know you very well?"

"Betty just knows me. Nothing else. I helped her out a few times because of her brother…: Like I said you were lucky to have her lead you to me, but don't make the same mistake twice in trusting in her.

Like I said trust in no one but this time you got lucky. That girl has her faults just like everyone else does. Now go on go back to bed."

"I want too, but I just can't seem to relax... I'm all up-tight, and I don't know why..." I robed the back of my neck saying.

"I know what will relax you. You need a good massage. I use to be a masseuse. Go lay down on the floor and I'll see what I can do to help you relax."

I trusted him and my neck was so stiff that I thought it was going to snap. I tossed a few couch pillow down on the floor to rest my head on, and went to lay on the floor stretched out upon my stomach.

He straddled himself over the back of my legs as I laid stretched out on the carpeted floor, and started to massage my neck and shoulders.

Those fingers of his worked their incredible magic putting me under their anesthetizing spell. Relaxing me tighten neck muscles, and tense nerves to the point my entire body became so relaxed

His stimulating fingers were so skillful they took possession over me. Suppressing any apprehensions, or fears as I unknowingly became increasingly more calmly submissive from the way he was making me feel letting his stimulating finger go where they wanted too.

Allowing him to message my entire body

I was in awe, being manipulated with insurmountable splendor being besieged with overwhelming apprehension that he might stop.

In an insatiable state of possession over wanting him to linger longer with what they were doing traumatically being besieged upon when they left where they were.

Leaving too taunt me elsewhere. Too heartlessly tantalize, my skin nerves, and muscles into tingling, twitching, and rippling scream out for them not to stop all over again.

I was a seventeen, year old naive girl who's never been touched like he was touching me. Experiencing revelations from the way he was so expertly manipulating my body.

Torturing me to the point beyond becoming relaxed causing every nerve and muscle to become hypersensitive to being touched

I wasn't mentally prepared for his level of attentiveness. His tactful fingers where provoking sensations that I having extreme trouble mentally as well as physically tolerating. Panicky wanting him to stop, but terrified with the thought over what might happen to me if he did.

Never have I ever experienced anything so madding. His masterful magical hands took total possession over any well of resistance to deny him the liberates he was lavishing upon me

His stimulating fingers never stopped. I was enthralled in the sublicenses of mindlessness allowing his masterful fingers too desensitize my entire body.

Finding myself opening my blurry eyes having to clear out the dizziness before them still somewhat dazzled stricken with the sun's rays bearing into them from the windows behind the sofa blinding me.

Rapidly blinking straining my blinding eyes to see more clearly Coming upon Tom's gorgeous blue eyes staring into mind facing me lying on his back beside me on the floor.

Physically and mentally still besieged with the most spectacular mind boggling experience I ever had in my entire life. Lying beside him struggling to regain some sort of composure aimlessly staring at him.

Being force to come to the realization over what just happened, and all I wanted to do was too revel in the benevolence of the mind boggling revaluations that I experienced from me trusting in him.

Smiling ingratiatingly literally thanking him for the moment I would never forget as long as I lived, speaking out to him.

"What ever happened to your philosophy?" I asked looking into his sparkling eyes glistening back into mind.

"I don't know...?" He bewilderingly replied with a confused expression upon his face."

This has never happened before...?"

"Now that I find hard to believe. You're too damn good at it not to be an expert at it..."

"Helen you're not upset over what just happened are you? You're over 18 I'm sure and I had no idea that you were…" He stopped abruptly not wanting to finish what he was asking me.

"You can't be serous?" I sarcastically rebutted." Of course I'm upset… wouldn't any girl be who's just lost her virginity… and no I'm not over eighteen! Close, but no cigar…"

You tricked me, and I was gullible enough to trust you… You took advantage of me. Just so you could have your way with me…

You lied, manipulated, and seduced me into submitting to your manly desires… damn right I'm upset…!"

"Helen I swear I never meant for anything like this to happen, I thought that you were the one ling to me about your age, and you weren't putting up any kind of an argument, or even attempted to stop me. I admit I'm partly to blame, but you can't expect me to take all the blame. However, I can fully understand why you should be upset, but regardless that it did there's nothing I can say, or do to change it, but to tell you that I'm glad that it did happen…

It was too incredible to believed… I can't bring myself to believe that I was the first to experience the sensationalism of being your first. Not even God himself could ever be so lavished upon by such a diving goddess as you…

Helen I realize that his is an awkward time to ask this, but seeing how the best thing in my life has already happened to me I feel I don't have anything to loss by asking.

Helen seeing how I have already hired you as my maid, and I'm most likely going to make an honest woman out of you and do the honorable thing by you. After you turn 18 that is but, until then I'll do my best to take really good care of you?"

"You mean so you can continue to do your manly thing, is that it?"

"Well yes of course. I mean the worse is obviously over, and I know you loved it as much as I did."

"What makes you say that?"

"Like I said you didn't even attempt push me off you, nor do you appear to be all that mad at me, and your eyes are sparkling and smiling at me. Face it Helen we really hit it off together, so why not when we could continue to have a bright enjoyable future together?

There's not that much of an age difference between us, and go. I'm already obsessed with overwhelming infatuation for you so who knows now far are relationship could progress. I'm only trying to be rational.

All you need to do is to tell me how you feel about the idea. I know you're upset right now over what just happened, but if you agree I promise that you'll never regret it as far as I'm concern.

We both felt it, are coming together goes beyond us just having sex together. We bonded together as one having sex is no longer a concern where we're concern"

"I want to think about it, but while I'm doing it how's about another stimulating massage… But! I want to be totally aware of your every move this time… And you damn will better be extremely gentle with me…

You sneaking up on me like you did, is leaving lingering repercussion over just how far thing went between us.

I'm not going to lie you I know how devastatingly wonderful if was, but I was a naive virtuous young girl before you open up all those incredibly sensational sensations that I've been missing out on. It's the aftermath of becoming adjusted to becoming a woman unprepared that I'm referring too, but don't be taking me for granted I'm still haven't decided just yet…"

His conniving philandering lips went straight for my still crusted over lips too lavishly kiss me. Ever so affectionately working his arousing lips up to my nose, ears than down to my neck, ears.

As if he was once again seductively attempting to inspire his desire to elevate me back into becoming respondent… By prompting me as if provoking me into submissively slid up around his neck passionately kissing him back

It was too incredible to believe. Me… The timid, inhibited, fearful girl was giving myself to a full grown man and I was loving it…!

I felt dominating powerful, and in supreme control over him, and it became magnificently spellbinding experiencing being liberated from all those apprehensions that bared me from unleashing the inner women that was lurking inside me beckoning to come forth, which made me feel all that more impulsive to find out the total me that I was emerging into.

CHAPTER 2

That morning and the rest of the next day. All I did was embellish myself in the magnificent splendor of exercising my authority over him by keeping him uncomfortably on edge over what I was going to decide, knowing that I held control over his future destiny.

Again naively acting extremely stupid not knowing how much he was to tolerate or just how dangerous he really was to be intimidating.

I couldn't believe it that being a woman could have such dominance over a man. Me being only 17 years' old who had nothing to offer him other than who I was, and where I was in my life.

Even though he was reaping the benefits of taking advantage of him to experiment with becoming a liberated women and him being so strong and so masculinity debonairly handsome, and not just some arrogant inconsiderate high school asshole that could never be have the man I was now dominating over.

Who was no longer so naive and had a hell of a lot of catching on what I missed out on by wanting to be all the women he could ever want and wanting him to appreciate the women he would never find himself losing his desire for.

I was thinking as an affectionate young girl thinking by what I was doing was the way he wanted me to respond to him while ignorantly believing I was doing it all for myself wanting to become emancipated from everything I believed in

Tom was nothing less that stupendous. Within those first 17 hours he denied himself, or me nothing,

In those spectacular fantastic hours, I took myself from a naive timid innocent girl into the women I thought he wanted me to be fore him

Where my apprehension started to emerge with aspirations over the way he was catering to my every whim, by not forcing me to stop, or encouraging me to at least slow down.

Obviously thinking that I wouldn't understand why he would want me to stop, and I would think of his doing so as a form of rejection. That would emotionally hurt me worse than I could ever do to myself physically.

Which might cause me to become spiteful against him, and react violently against him where doing so might create a disturbance that could bring the cops, and he couldn't afford getting involved with them. By getting himself caught having sex with a 17-year-old girl.

My reasoning was also giving me the impression that was also totally opposite of what I was assuming that was prompted me feeling that I was. With me being the aggressor between the two of us.

The impression he was projecting suggesting that what he was doing. Was as if he wasn't never going to be able to make love to another woman again.

Like as if he was a dying man, but not knowing when he was going to die and every moment he spent with me was going to be his last.

There was something disturbingly unnerving about him that kept me on edge with the haunting thoughts that I was never going to see him again, if I let him get out of my sight.

Little did Helen know was, what she was opening myself up for, and little by little until she finally came to discover why he was acting the way he was, when he was alone with me.

Within the span of those first seven, hours they shared together Helen experienced sides of him, as well as myself.

That left her feeling fearfully apprehensive over that she might never see him again, and the closer she became the more she felt the time they were sharing was going to be short lived, and she was going to find myself abandoned, and hating myself for letting him out of my arms.

* * * *

After their first full day past and things started to settle down between the two of them. Helen came to feel more relaxed about her fearing that he was going to abandoned her as soon as he got the chance to do so.

She came to express herself more openly exposing more and more about herself while trying to connect closer to Tom who was very discreet about telling her anything about himself but, making a point on empathizing on his being able to come and going freely without having to explain himself which she didn't mind so much.

However, what she did mind was him giving her directions over what to do if when he left and didn't come back after five, days.

That he wanted her to take an envelope that he'll leave for her in the top dresser drawer after cleaning the apartment thoroughly making sure to remove any evidence that she was living in his apartment including her finger prints and the clothes she was while she stays at his place, and leave.

Saying that when he did return he would find her, but to remember everything he taught her up until such a time that it might happen.

* * * *

The days became more days during which Tom kept making calls putting off having to go back to work and ordering out for food to eat while we lounged about the apartment accessibly dressed just in case the mood hit either one of us.

Until a week pasted where the two, of us took a lot of time to get to know each where we pretty much kept to ourselves rather than him taking me out to meet his some of his friends.

Him keeping me to himself didn't annoy the hell out of me as much as him refusing to address my concerns of the possibility of him getting me pregnant.

Where he adamantly expresses his lack of concern, saying. Stop worrying so damn much once you turn 18 I'll be making an honest woman out of you."

His bullheadedness annoyed the hell out of me when it came to addressing my concerns wanting him to wear protection was to say that least nerve-racking as hell on me.

I was only going to be eighteen. There was no way I wanted to become a mother. Hell I didn't even know anything about life myself let alone bring a child into the world.

I wanted to enjoy discovering what it was like to enjoy living my life, I wanted to socialize, and party, and go places and do all the things I could never do before in my life.

I had enough of taking care of someone else and depriving myself, and I was loving my new life just as it was.

Besides I send what a few of the girl I went to school with and what happen to them once they got themselves pregnant. There was no way I was going to let that happen to me.

Where Tom hated wearing protection and liked being spontaneous reactive and once he started putting his moves on me there was no way I was going to say no.

Once Tom started taking me out with him it was always us together except when he had to go to work or away for a couple days where he left me home alone to do whatever I wanted to do.

The last thing I didn't want was to go anywhere near the neighborhood where I lived. So I spent most of my time taking care of the apartment, shopping for food, and anything else I could afford which I was not only getting pay as his maid but also getting a spending allotment that wasn't a lot but was enough to go out to buy myself trinkets, and clothes and get my hair done.

In the weeks that followed I came to find out about what Tom was involved in. During our conversation he attempted to prepare me for when he did with those he introduces me to, e to be his friends.

From the way he was elaborating of how dangerous his life style was, and thrilling as I was finding it, but ignorantly not accepting the hazardous that went along with it.

Mainly because I never realized the risks and dangers involved because Tom always came home and was always there for me when I needed and wanted him to be.

I mentally separated his way of life from my own and never really pressured him to tell me anything about what he was doing.

One would think that underneath all that sensitively what was really lurking was the devil himself including me.

Who was feared by his enemies, respected by those who knew him, and wanted by the authorities for heinous unthinkable crimes not excluding murder.

Tom was the living epitome of a hardcore gangster deeply immersed in the syndicate who even showed me one of his guns that he carried with him even, while he was out with me without me knowing about.

Now that really frighten the hell out of me, but I must admit I did find it rather comforting as well. Knowing that he could protect me under any circumstances.

Tom's life style was having an excitingly fascinating effect on me and I was finding myself enthusiastically wanting to take an active part in it, and when we were alone he would actually let me hold his gun.

I had to admit holding it would send chills throughout my entire body, and when he even let me squeeze the trigger it would cause me to have an orgasm. I mean actually hold the power of life and death in your hands was nothing less than accelerating.

Especially when I actually squeezed back on the trigger at time just fantasying about experiencing firing a bullet from it would induce me to experience a massive orgasm.

All the while I was with Tom I was like a little kid in a candy shop never getting enough and wanting more. I was living a dream world obsessed with wanting him in any way I could have him...

When he made a woman out of me he aroused a dormant entity within me that lied unknowingly in waiting to be awaken.

* * * *

During the first serval weeks I spent with Tom. I came to love the man I was beginning to find out so much about.

What I was finding so remarkable about our togetherness was that I was still maintaining his total undivided attention and that he protectively making sure that nothing would happen to me. Tom was by no means pussy whipped. He was however a one-woman man, but not in the least over bearing, but like all man impulsive inspirational which I most certainly was finding provocatively endearing about him.

But, always demanding when I go out to always let him know where I was going or where he could find me if he needed to get in touch with me, and if I wasn't where I told him I would be I should call him and tell him where I'm going.

Tom trusted me even knowing I was in position of putting him behind bars, and the fact that I was finding out more about him than anyone else ever did.

Over time I even learnt a lot about Tom's previous life and all that he had to endured to get where he was in his life.

That he was on his own from the age of ten. Running away from his father who despised the ground he walked on and sought to even kill him twice.

Who spent a great deal of his life on his own stealing, and sleeping in abandoned houses learning how to survive living on the streets.

Once by tossing him out of a second story window when he was 4 years old and again by trying to beat him to death when he was six, years old.

Tom was a loner who trusted in no one, or cared about anyone but himself, but who would do anything for those closest to him. Which only amounted to a few people including me.

He had no qualms about doing what he had to do, and yes, extremely unscrupulous in mature, as well as sadistic when it came to getting even.

Yet he was the nicest person I ever met and the most trusting, and caring person too where I was concern. He said once.

"Never believe what anyone say about someone else. Always judge for yourself. Give them one shot at you, and warn them that they better not miss, and say nothing more.

Anything more will only encourage them to find out what you meant. Always keep them skeptical of you, and uncertain about if they want to risk finding out how you might react."

Tom was the only person I ever knew that was involved with the syndicate. What I didn't know was what it entailed to be involved with a criminal organization such as the syndicate, but the more I learnt about Tom, and his involvement with the syndicate. The more I became aware of that he appeared to be the exception within the organization.

He tried to make himself appear like just one of the guys, but there was something about him that seeped through that persona to expose a much different personally hidden side of him.

I got the impression he was someone that no one really wanted to become involved with. Like as if doing so meant something that could be very detrimental to them personally.

He loved walking, and when we did talk he never came right out and said anything directly. There was always a logical philosophy behind what he said, and at times when he didn't know how to express himself, or he would become very long winded.

He would just walk away as if an alarm would go off in his head catching himself. His introverted personally made it extremely easy for him not to care, and to be heartless cruel not to mention sadistically torture some.

Tom never made it past the sixth grade so he wasn't very well educated and when he talked he himself had to know what he was talking about, but when he did he did so very intelligently.

As for talking about himself. He was very careful not to mention anything that would shed any light on what went on in his life and stood behind every word he said.

Even with me he was very careful not to divulge too much, and damn if he didn't have one hell of a tempter, and what even made it worse was, that he was extremely over protective of me.

Tom never carried a weapon with him because, he was the weapon until I came into his life. He practiced at being the ultimate weapon daily at hours on end.

Inside his private apartment across the hall from the one we were living in, and that I would stay in when he was working as a bouncer, or had to go away for a few days.

At time when we would walk together, and actually got out of the car to do so in some of the most dangerous sections of the city.

Where he would meet up with some of his friends, and discus personal business between each other. Knowing that if he left me alone with another of their friends I would be taken care of and respected

Those who recognized him referred to him as Angle man. I asked him why they called him that. He replied.

"When I was young I had this guardian angel who looked out after me. Me being the stupid bullheaded kid that I was ... I got my butt stumped pretty regularly" He empathized stressing upon.

" I just couldn't seem to run from anything, or to stay down or run away from anyone for that matter.

No matter what the odds were against me, and I guess that's why this guardian angel adopted me because it felt sorry for me.

When I got hurt those who hurt me had accidents, or something would always happen to them. It didn't take long before word got around that I had myself a guardian angel."

"Tom aren't you scared actually walking in these hazardous places?"

"Yes, very much so. One would have to be totally out of their mind not to be, but fear is my Allie. I can only die once. Fear is a state of mind, when someone fears losing something. Where I died years ago, and had nothing to lose until you enter my life.

Nothing matters to me other than the fact that I'm here, and the way I see it. They can't kill a dead person.

Chop me up, break me into paces, and if they leave me alive afterwards All those paces will come back together again for the sole purpose of comforting those that were stupid enough to let me live.

I walked and I stood alone. I judge no one. But be it may if they want to judge me wrongly. I'm not invincible by any means I just don't care.

By all right I should have died years ago, or I could have, and don't even realize it. I bare the scares that could have made it so, but I still live.

I overcome death not knowing what it was until I was nine and I was befriended by a very special person in my life. Where I was forced to bare the meaninglessness of life seeing her dying before my eyes.

Forcing me to look upon death as an unscrupulous meaningless function of life as it robed me of mine and made my life meaningless to live.

"What about me?"

"Why do you think I'm taking you with me? I want all to know who you are. I want all eyes to see, and honor you for who you're, and how proud you make me just to be seen with you, but don't be expecting me to fight for you.

I fight only for myself and my convictions, and I honestly believe it's those convictions that resurrected that guardian angel who even I don't want to having anything to do with.

I lay no claim on anyone or thing not even you. Things never lasted with me they come and go so they're meaningless to me. That's why I can't lay claim to you.

You belong to yourself to which I'll stand proud beside. Where honor, or prestige, have no meaning in this day and age.

As for disgrace I've face that so many times that I had to become two faced. One for losing, and one for myself.

No one seen to care which one I show, they're going to do what they want to do and in return I'll do what I have to do to face myself when I look at myself in the mirror.

"Tom you're only one person what can one do against many if something did happen to you, what who happen to me?

You can't expect someone else to protect me the way you do or even care about me in the same way you do. There's never going to be another you.

You were a loner. That's no longer the case, but that still leaves us both alone with no one, but each other.

Just because you took my virginity didn't mean that I wanted to become a part of your life. I chose to become so. I wish I could honestly say I did so out of love for you, but I can't. I still don't even know what real love is like yet.

What I do know is all I can think about is wanting to be with you, and I don't want us being together to ever stop, but I've to except the fact that it can at any time, and I will be alone again and the thought of that happening is an unbearable one to bare."

"There's an old saying a very wise person once told me. He said, though you're one where's there's always going to be one amongst many. Where many are also but one amongst many, who are one of many, but of a few.

Where them you become the many as you stay joined with the powers of I, me, and yourself. The forces of which are invincible when they're combined together as one came make the many become but a few and a few but one thereby being placed on equal ground.

Which are the forces that exist in all of us, but only a few know how to represent themselves knowing how to call upon what they already have in them.

The power of me. Refers to fear, the power of I means summoning your inner strength, and the power of I is combining the three together and applying them to overcome the many by the way one stands in defense of himself form an unbeatable force without fear, pain, or rage, but concentrated about on one objective, death itself. Where there's no life.

There's no fear of death or dying. If left alive to rise up again will only bring about their inevitable defeat by doing so.

You're fearing the unknown needlessly. It hasn't happened yet, and until it does live life for all you can get out of it.

You're young you've your whole life ahead of you. You've yet too have lived those years that have already past for you. You can't live in fear over your future for it is unknown, as for death that's the only sure thing that can come from life.

Your concern is well founded but premature. Knowing you the way I do I know you'll do just fine without me. If it ever came to that. As I would want you to.

I can't guarantee anything other than I'm here for you now, and will continue to be for as long as our destinies for it to do so last, but I can do no more than that.

You also fail to comprehend the meaning about what I meant when I said I will only fight for myself. As long as we're also regarded as one my fear of death does not exist. because I welcome it as another form of my existence.

That if we are meant to be together we will in death itself now that we found each other. We live together so shall we be existing so in death.

Sure of course I'll do all I can to provide for you if I'm around to do so, but beyond that both of our lives are uncertain, and neither you nor I can dote on apprehensions. It will only drive a wedge between us that shouldn't be there.

We exist in time who we do it is entirely up to us on one but us is entitled to violated infringe upon what's ours.

That where I am, and where I walk is how I want to spend my time I do not tread to share my time with anyone else but those I chose too, so they should not dare tread in mind. "

I didn't find out what he meant by what he said until sometime later when I actually saw that horrifying face of death on Tom's face.

It's a face I'll never forget even upon my own dying day. It was such a grotesque face that would terrify the living hell of anyone who dared to look upon it, but when they see it. It's too late... Death would already be upon them.

ARTHUR RICHTER

CHAPTER 3

I've been going with Tom going on 6 weeks now. Tom had to leave town for a few days and I became bored and decided to go out, and do some shopping.

I was on Broadway doing some shopping. When a friend of my mother's spotted me and called the police.

Where I was arrested and taken to the police station and questioned by the police as to where I was for the past six, weeks, and where I got the $300.00 I had in my purse.

Then they asked me to account for how I could be wearing a $200.00 outfit that I was wearing that Tom bought for me from Fredericks of Hollywood.

They kept grueling me for hours until in inadvertently Tom's name just slipped out. The detective questioning me nearly had a heart attack when he heard Tom's name.

Immediately the detective replied back.

"This guy Tom did he happen to be known as the phantom?"

"I don't know who you could be referring to by that name, and I happen to knew a lot of guys by the name of Tom.

Just by looking at me and how well I was being kept. Just as much as told them that I was ling through my teeth.

Because I became so complacent too living in Tom's apartment. I mean nothings ever happen that would have cause me to be conscientious about following through with going to the next apartment.

Even when I forgot to do it, then remembered what I was supposed to do nothing ever happened. It just didn't appear to be all that accentual to bother with all the time.

So I ignored clearing up the apartment we were living in and ignored going through the hassle of removing my finger prints thinking that my being hired as his maid should be enough to account for any that might show up.

What shocked me even more was how they could have found out where I was at after constantly asking me where I was staying.

They said that they went to his Tom's apartment, and even took finger prints determining that I was there, but they didn't know for how long.

Until they questioned the neighbors and asked around showing my picture. Getting several to say that they spotted me being around for some time now going in and out of Tom's apartment.

Tom was still gone, and I was never involved with the police before, and they were scaring the hell out of me, threatening me with reform school.

Where to me that meant they taking Tom away from me. There was no way I was going to let them separated us.

So I broke down and told them what Tom told me to tell them. That I was only working as his maid, and continued to refuse to tell them where I was really living, when I wasn't working for him.

Like a stupid fool that I was. I didn't find out how the cops found out was by the key too Tom's apartment. It has the apartment building address and the apartment number on it. They discovered it when they went through my purse.

I unwittingly gave Tom up to the cops. The more I was opening my mouth the more charges they were compiling against him, and they weren't about to stop until they squeezed everything they could out of me. So that they could put him away for as long as they could.

They had my mother collaborating with them having her questioning me about my whereabouts.

Always crying asking me why, and who else was involved in helping me stay away from home where I was loved by my family.

The cops had no problem with proving most of the charges against Tom but their primary charge that they arrested Tom on was for contributing to my delinquency, but they wanted more. They wanted to nail him for statutory rape.

They got my mother's permission to have me examined by a doctor to find out if I was a virgin or not, or if I had recent sexual intercourse.

It just so happened the previous evening before Tom left. Tom and I really got sexually involved, and even though they discovered that I wasn't a virgin, they weren't able to confirmed that I was recently sexually involved without me admitting that it was with Tom or not. They needed me too confirm it, and I wasn't saying anything.

I told my mother as well as the cops that my virginity was my business and for all they knew I could have been having sex with myself using something.

Luckily for me Tom was out of town already for a day and even though they could determine that it was, had sex.

They couldn't determine with who, and seeing how I was no longer a virgin, and not telling who got to me. They couldn't prove a damn thing against Tom

I repeatedly denied living with Tom. I said that I went to visit him frequently because I was working for him as his maid, and yes, we just talked, but emphatically denied that he ever touched me.

I even went as far as resorting to making myself out a prostitute in order to explain how I could afford living away from home for so long, and for the clothes I was wearing. Saying that Tom would even feed me at time while we talked amongst each other.

Telling them that Tom never knew that I was a runaway, and was under the assumption that I was twenty, years old, and that was the extent of our friendship.

Who I ask to hold onto my clothes at his place until I got one of my own, and would be able to move out from my friend's place, which I wouldn't even tell the cops where that was.

No matter how hard they tried they couldn't break me down. There was no way I was going to tell them anything simply because I was in love with Tom.

I spent enough time with Tom to know that all the cops could do to me was to send me home, Where I would just runaway again mainly because they couldn't prove that I committed any crime they could charge me with.

Other than running away from home, and due to the fact that I was only mouths away from becoming eighteen, and legally an adult that.

Where they couldn't threaten me with reform school. Even though they threatened to send me to one until I was eighteen, made me feel uncertain that they couldn't.

They showed me Tom's police record. It was over ten, pages thick. Suspicion for this, and that, but no conviction.

They depicted him as a cheap thug, a syndicate hood, and a killer, and a beater of helpless children, and women, and even accused him of being a rapist as well.

I still refused to tell them anything. Nothing they could tell me could turn me against Tom. Even though Tom never exposed me to what he actually did. I knew what he was capable of, but only when he was provoked to defend himself like at work.

As far as him being a rapist. Tom didn't have to resort to raping any women before I came into his life and most assuredly didn't afterwards.

Knowing Tom, the way I did I knew that he could have had any women he wanted, and had more women than he could possibly handle hitting on him. That he didn't need to rape any women.

I was taken to juvenile hall where I was released into my mother's custody. Two, days later word came to me by way of the detective who questioned me telling that Tom was arrested for contributing, and saying that I was going to have to testify for the state.

I defiantly said that I wouldn't, and they couldn't force me to lie for them. Knowing with the connections that Tom had he would get out of it. I mean he was involved with the syndicate. They weren't going to let anything happen to him not for all he has done for them.

What I didn't know was that Tom was already out of jail and out looking for me. He never knew where I lived, and my mother and 3 brothers stood guard over me. So that I couldn't get away to go to his place, and every time I called him he was never answering his phone. Possibly knowing that he could risk anyone knowing that we were involved.

I was still only seventeen, and the cops were really out to get him, and all they would need is a romantic connection to nail him.

DISPLACEMENT INTENT

* * * *

It was Friday nearly a week since I was arrested. I waited until my mother left for work and the boys were settled in for the night then snuck out of my bedroom window.

It was 1 AM. I was heading for the bus stop heading for Tom's apartment. When a Pontiac convertible come squealing out from the curve, and came to a screeching halt in front of me. Blocking me from crossing the street as I stood at the corner.

The passenger door flow open, and Tom's voice came billowing out shouting out at me.

"Come on get in dammit...!"

I didn't hesitate to get in. With him not waiting until I closed the door before he sped off causing the door to slam shout by itself.

I was so happy to see him I couldn't stop from leaping across the seat to excitedly hug and kiss him. Expressing my enthusiastic joy of being back with him again.

He drove to a secluded spot and parked. I wanted to climb all over him I was so excited, but all he wanted to do was to talk and held me at bay at arm's length. Wanted to know everything that I told the cops.

I told him everything that happened, and all I said then asked him if he was mad at me.

He yelled back." Hell! Yes, I am...! I could ring your beautiful neck...! That's how passed off I am...!"

He reached out to me taking me in his aggressive arms hugging me to him whispering in my ear.

"You damn fool... Can't you see that I love you..."

That was all I needed to hear to forcefully pull him down on top of me." Frantically crying out against his cheek." My God Tom... I love you so, so, so very much. I'm so sorry..."

Anxiously reached down pulling up the bottom of my dress wrapping my legs around his waist, grabbing hold of his neck. Pulling his gorgeous face and lips down upon mind kissing him with longing passion.

Only to have him breaking my lips embrace, too rise up upon his bracing arms above me. To look down into my desiring eyes as he tried to keep a stern expression upon his face. Speaking out to me with a fearful longing in his voice.

"You better damn well be sorry... But you're not going to be as sorry as you're going to be if you ever try to leave me again...

You're coming back home with me... Do you've any idea how much I suffered not having you around to take care of me?"

He barked at me, while not attempting to show how much he really missed me, by not attempting to show his love for me.

When all I wanted him to do was to hold me in his loving arms again, and not having him infuriating me more than I already was over being separated from him.

"Oh, I see... So all I am is a maid to you now, is that it... Is that why you missed me...? I obliged him by annoyingly barking back at him by not patronizing his manly ego. Pushing him up off me by his hips. Defiantly not excepting his position over me speaking out.

"Well, whatever the reason I'm back now where I belong... I'll settle for that even though you came to find me with something else in mind. That I'm not willing to except for an answer why it took you so damn long to find me..."

I hunched up my pelvic region up above the seat wanting him to remove my panties... Wanting him to once again unite us in that unbreakable bond that rejoined our hearts, minds, and very souls to come together as one. Whispered into his ear.

"Just don't let this go to that swollen head of yours I'm only fed up with being denied. You still owe me for services rendered that you've been ignoring to pay for far too long, and while I'm at it. I'm not about to go doing anymore windows, and seeing how you're being stubborn and obviously bullheaded about trying to make so sort of nerve-racking point.

I want a rise...! For all my pain and anguish I've been put through because of my love for you. I aggressively exercised my promissory rights, and took matters into my own hands.

"Now are you just going to continue tormenting me, or do what you promised me. Too do the honorable thing by me? You owe me big time and I want you back where you belong."

It was the most incredibly outrageous experience we ever shared together it was that ballistic ally intensifying and nothing less than veraciously invigorating.

We laid holding each other in each other's loving arms panting hyperventilating into each other's ear as we both basket in each other's sweat struggling to regain some sort of composure to stop the insatiable madness going on between us.

With me gruelingly refusing to release him from my interlocked ankles. Regretfully feeling myself coming back to the present. Having to accept the grin reality that we're going to have to have no choice but continue to be separated. Solemnly speaking out into his ear.

"Honey I can't go home with you. The police will arrest you again, but there's nothing in this world that is going to keep me from seeing you. I've the devil himself, and I'm in sole possession of him, and I'm not about to let him get away.

It's been hell on me this past week. I don't think that it was possible for me to survive being separated more than a couple days without you...

You've no idea how I've longed for this moment, and how unbearable it has been on me not being able to reach out to you I've been kept prisoner in my own house and watched constantly by the cops just waiting for you to show up and to catch us together.

I've seen and heard things about you that should horrify the hell out of me where the only thing that matters to me is being with you and feeling your love surging throughout my entire body.

This is where I belong holding you in my arms feeling your love for me embellishing me with the strength to endure the seconds I'm going to be separated from you.

Knowingly knowing the risk of having to let you go. Not knowing what's happening to you is only going to make my torment that much more unbearable."

"Helen I'm here to take you back home with me... I'm not going to let some two-bite cops come between us. It's bad enough I have to leave you at times... This long term shit isn't going to hatch it..."

"No Tom... Tom you must listen to me." I rebelliously took a stand against him." I'm not going to risk having you wind up in some jail cell again, or taken away from me any longer that possible. I just won't be able to live without you. I won't I tell you... I won't! I hysterically cried out squeezing my ankles tighter around his waist.

"Now you listen to me dammit! I'm going to be the one who's going to decide if I'm going to go home with you or not, and I promise you I will figure out a way for us to continue to be together, but we're going to have to do it legally where they can never separate us ever again or use me as an excuse to arrest and but you in any prison cell."

"Helen you could marry me."

"What did you say...?!" I dumbfounding blurted out asking not believing he would even say such a ridiculous thing. Knowing that it was virtually impossible knowing my mother would never agree to me marrying him

"I said you could marry me... Will you marry me...?"

"Yes...! Yes...! Oh, my God! Yes...!" I zealously answered him trying to maintain my composure from not busting out into tears of joy.

Kissing him all over his gorgeous face. Rekindling his still simmering flame of passion excitedly flaring up inside me excitedly jostling about beneath him.

"Honey it was going to happen eventually any ways. I know I said that I was going to a great many times already, but I honest and truly always meant it, and even more so now."

"Goddamn you Tom! You sure can pick the awkwardness time to start getting serious on me. You know damn well I would do anything to become your wife... Yes, dammit yes...!" I vigorously became more aggressively responsive.

"Now calm down Helen there's still your age to consider... I got this plan... So give me time to tell you. Before you get us both all worked up again." He grabbed hold of my hips holding me at bay so that he could tell me what his plan was.

"I was thinking that I could play up to your mother. Once I turn on my charm she won't be able to resist me... I'll get her to consent to us getting married along with your help."

"No good. She's read your police record, and beside there's no way I'm going to let you anywhere near my mother. Especially with that captivating charm of yours.

Least of all anything else... You belong solely to me now... I'm going to be your wife, and I'm claiming sole custody.

My mother has been without my father since I was 10 years old, and she's the last person I would trust you with. No way...!

By the way you really didn't do all those things the cops suspect you of doing, did you? I mean by all right if you did you should be behind bars.

Seeing that we are on the subject I would like to know just where is that going to put me on that list of accomplices of yours?

Now when it's obviously far too late exclude me, seeing how you already got me involved way over your head with you?"

"I did nothing they can prove so let's leave it like that..."

"Tom they say that you actually killed people..."

"Dammit Helen! Just let it go...!" He annoyingly spoke out trying to rise up out of my arms.

"Oh, no you don't...!" I held onto him stopping him from going anywhere." Angry, or not you're staying right where you are." I tighten my locking hands and legs about him." Now you're going to stay right where you're, or I'll start screaming rape...!

It's time that you realize just who's the boss here... As for what you supposedly did I don't want to think about it, as for what you're going to do. If you truly love me, you'll make sure nothing comes between us to separate us."

"You don't understand what you're asking of me. I owe a lot of people more than I could ever repay. They were there for me when I needed them. I'm obligated Helen I just can't walk away...

You know so very little about my life. That if you ever found out you would have nothing but contempt and loathing for me.

There's no way I can just leave. It just doesn't happen in my line of work, and even I could I don't even know if it's possible for me to change. I just can't up and create a whole new life for myself and leave my past behind me."

"Then it is all true. You're a syndicate hood?"

"No, Helen I'm no hood. Hoods get caught, I don't. I'm a specialist, and I'm telling you there's no way I'm going to get caught at anything I do.

Honey I told you what it would be like. I even protected you from finding out how it was like out on the streets, and gave you everything you wanted.

You've to understand it's not anything like the way you heard about. It's a very tough way of life that has its risk yes, but so does any other way of life. Which I don't want you to ever have to experience, or become a part of.

That's why expose you to so many. Knowing that once I presented you, if anything happens to me you would have someone looking out after you.

I not only see people for what they really are, and have to deal with the sort of life that you could have begun a part of by protecting you from the way it's really like.

I see it and live it the way it really is with people the way they really are. I've been doing so since I was ten, years old. I don't know any other way of life."

"Tom none of that crap matters to me. You're not the only one who had to deal with hardships in their lives, you did what you had to do. I get that, but you fail to see that you're all that matters to me, and I want you just the way you're… What I want you to tell me is. Can you give me all that you are without the fear of something happening to you?"

"Honey you've to be realistic about this. No one can promise that. I'm not immortal I can be hurt just like you or anyone else.

A lot of people invested a lot of time, and money in seeing to it that I live a long prosperous life because I made promises, and committed myself to them.

I know what I'm doing. I'm not no fly by night independent, or thug that doesn't have the brains, or the ability to know what they're doing. I've been groomed and extensively trained for the life style I'm living.

I'm a professional and I don't do anything without not knowing the risks involved. Knowing that even the simplest thing could get me caught."

"I'm not just talking about that… I'm talking about you. I'm the one who holds you in my arms. As you tremble, shake, and when you wake up in a cold sweat in the middle of the night.

I've no doubt that you'll survive when you're out doing your thing, but how long can you survive being tormented, and terrorized by the memories of what you did, or do, and what happened to you during. I see the scars that you bare but, I'm not the one who has to bare the pain, and anguish from them before something mentally happens to you...

You're being haunted by what you are doing because you have on one you can trust to unburden yourself of all that you're carrying around inside you that what let you forget their faces, and what happened.

Honey as much as I love you. Even I don't want to shear that part of your life with you but how can I not knowing that every time you leave me you might never come back? You just said it yourself that you're not immortal and I have seen with my own eyes how you have been hurt.

Then there's me and those you hurt, or whatever else you might have done to them. Wanting to revenge themselves.

I love you I want to devote my life to making you happy I don't want to live in constant fear that someone is going to come looking for you, and find me, or that you might piss someone off who you once worked for. Where I've to live in fear of my life as well."

"It's not like you're making it out to be. It's just a job, that pays very handsomely I might add. As for fearing about things that haven't happened yet, it's totally stupid to do so. I could just as easily get kill by a thousand other ways.

Alright I grant you it's a dirty hazardous job, but like I said before. It's all I know how to do. What sort of life would that be for you? Having a know nothing guy not being able to provide for you...? You've to let me do what I do best. It's a job that I don't have to advertise that I'm damn good at.

Honey I want are life together to be a happy glorious one. What could I possibly give you in way of comfort as I do right now only running a minimal amount of risk.

Hell cops run more of a risk to get themselves hurt or killed than I do. I'm in control because I'm the only one who knows what, and when I'm going to do anything, and knowing ahead what I'll be walking into.

I'm a sixth grade dropout from school. I've no skills, or training in anything else than I was trained to do. I live most of my life learning to be proficient at what I do and I live out of sight in amongst the common person. Hell I even work at an honest job that's riskier than what I do on the side.

I want to give you everything that you so richly deserve. I'm the first to admit that you do deserve better than me, but I'm still not all I can be.

I'm still learning where I don't have much further to go. Where I'll only be called upon for something special. The situation I'm in now is only temporary.

Just give me time, and I'll put you in a mansion with servants waiting on you. Adoring you with diamonds, furs, a new car even... Shear elegance will be yours...

I'll make you rich beyond your dreams, and all I ask in return is your love, and to never worry. I'll never let anything happen to you.

As for me I'm not about to let anything happen to me now that I've you. Believe in me Helen that's all I ask..."

"Alright Tom, but I swear if anything happens to you I'll ring your damn neck...! Just don't involve me in anything you do.

I don't want to know or hear about it, and if you get put in jail. Don't be expecting me to come visit you, and not wanting to drag you out with my own bare hands myself."

"I understand dear, but you will send me cigarettes won't you...? After all you're going to be the one holding all the money, and cigarettes are money in prison, so I hear."

"Not funny... Besides what good is money without you to spend it on me...? Now that you got me to go along with your life style now. I want you to reciprocate by letting me handle the mess I got you into by doing the following.

You're going to start coming to my home and visit me. You're going to court me dear heart, and love it. My mother is very old fashion in her ways. You'll pick me up, and bring me back home at a decent hour, and you'll be polite, dignified, and tolerate my three, brothers.

By the time you get into court you'll be a known contributor to my delinquency. Where no judge would ever convict you, if I walk in wearing an engagement ring... If you get my meaning...?"

"Your one smart girl dearest."

"You bet I am and don't you ever forget it, but you can be assured I'm not going to stop trying to change are situation.

I want you home with me. Not out doing whatever it is you do, but you're determined to make are life a rich and rewarding one.

Where I'm not going to lie to you. I want it to be that way myself. I just hope that it doesn't become a hardship on us until things do change."

"Honey I've been doing it since I was 12 years old I know how to handle myself, and if something happens just like what happen to me. That's what I've an attorney for."

"I'm sure that you are able to handle yourself legally yes, but there are also other ways for something to happen to you without me finding out about it. It's the not knowing that's going to make a nerve-racking out of me."

"Honey you can be assured about one thing. No one knows who I am, or where I am. Like I said, I work strictly by myself, and only take on what I know I can handle, and live within my means, and I even have myself a job.

Honey I'm a shadow who's never seen or heard. Who's known only by a few by one name and it's not the angle, it's by the name of the phantom, and there's only way one I can be called upon.

If anything does ever happen to me get hold of my attorney by the name of Phillip, I'll give you his number. Just tell him that the Phantom is in trouble he'll do the rest.

As far as anything else is concern. You will know by the code's we're going to set up between us. In the event that I should contact you by phone, and give it to you, and if the worst might happen I'm sure you will hear about it, but this is not the time to start thinking about that.

Honey, all we need is time to get everything together where we will both feel comfortable when either of us are apart from each other. What do you think...?"

"Well I know what you think you're capable of doing. As for up to now however you're going to have to show me that your man enough to finish what you started. Where I might add you are leaving a lot to be desired in the way of inspiration...

How long are you just going to linger and boast about your past accomplishments, or have you lost the ambition to pursue beyond your limitations, or maybe you're harboring deeply embedded feelings that I'm not aware of...?

"No way I'm quite content in gloating from egotistical grander right where I am. Knowing that I'll have a lifetime to ravel in the rewards of my greatest achievement. That of falling in love with you.

There's no greater honor than feeling the beating thumbing heartbeat, pulsating with the love of a compassionate women... It's time like this that I'm proud to be the recipient of such an auspicious honor such as I'm receiving

"You're quite the con-artist... You'll say anything to get me to bare the weight of your laziness. But if you're just going to bottle there and gloat. The least you could do is give me your acknowledgment in some form of gratitude.

That you're appreciating my effort to make you so very comfortable, and it's not doing it by just having you gloatingly smirking from ear to ear.

Now just what do you intend to do about the situation you placed us both in...?"

"Well seeing how I contributed so much I can't see how I could do anything but to take advantage of it.

But you must excuse me I seemed to have misplace something momentary, but I'm sure I'll find it if I search around some... Now please bear with me if I seem to be having a bit of a problem..."

"Yes..., Yes..., Please do search all you want... Allow me to help you if it will speed things up faster... Oh, yes... faster is working marvelously..."

I reached up clutching onto his neck giving him the insensitive he need to take up a more briskly search hastening to speed up his efforts in locating whatever it was he appeared to have lost.

DISPLACEMENT INTENT

* * * *

In the weeks that followed living with Tom wasn't by any means easy, physically or otherwise. He had to have his own way and I couldn't say no.

He had it set in his mind he wasn't going to deny me anything, and that he was a man of his word and wasn't going to let anything happen to him.

Even though I never thought of myself as anyone special he made me feel privileged to be loved by him

Sure I was gorgeous and I was giving him everything it was in my power to give him. Sexually, emotionally, and supportably always being there for him, but there was so much that I wasn't able to give him in ways of my moral support.

I hated what he was, and what he was doing to others, but at the same time I loved the man with all my heart and soul and he loved me and he was always coming home to me.

Even though I kept on ling to myself, saying that nothing else mattered, and I didn't care about anyone else as long as he came back to me.

Knowing it was wrong of me not to care, only carrying about no one but myself always, but always wanting to know what he did when he did come back, but not wanting to hear, knowing how hearing about it would affect me personally.

One eventually comes to be able to ignore, and just except. What is, for what it is. Until they come to the point where thinking about others seems to just dissipate from one's mind, and life itself appears to be moral.

It's strange how one's mind works, and how easy it is to just shut everyone else out of one's private world. As long as it doesn't disrupt that person's life style.

Except that is when he doesn't call, or shows up, or is late. Or when someone wearing a cheap suit comes knocking on the door. With you always having to be fearful of why, or if that someone is coming for you, or they're the cops coming to arrest someone.

It wasn't the easiest way of life to have to adjust too, but if one loves someone deeply enough it become livable.

Where one, learns how to live sneaking around to enjoy and appreciate the pleasures one's ill-gotten gains can bestow upon them right under everyone noses even the cops living in alternate world one being the life of the phantom.

CHAPTER 4

Three, more weeks past during which Tom kept coming over to the house with him turning on his charm. It took a hell of a lot of kissing up to my mother, but he was gradually breaking my mother down to where her resentment towards him started to dissipate.

She really hated and despised him at first, and even threatened to call the cops on him if he didn't leave her family alone.

Where it took a hell of a lot of influence on my part to convince her that what she was doing was pointless.

That calling the cops was pointless because he was only a friend trying to come to visit me. Who. was making certain to stay totally visible all the time.

Knowing the way, she obviously felt about him, and seeing how I was living in the house, and letting him come visit me there wasn't very much she could legally do to bar him from coming to see me. If he stood out on the sidewalk and I went out to meet him.

She didn't like it one damn bit that I stood up against her over the likes of some guy who must have taken advantage of me.

Even though I told her repeatedly that Tom never touched me. That he was being wrongfully prosecuted for something he never did. That all he was, was a friend to me.

One who I didn't want to lose as a friend, so I was going to continue to see him. If he wants to see me.

Convincing her that I was going to continue to defy her where Tom was concern, and that if I felt that he was only coming to visit me was so he could have manipulated me that I'll be the first to tell him to get lost, and would call the cops myself.

It took some time but eventually the sidewalk became the front steps, that lead eventually for him to be allowed to actually enter the house, and sit in the living room.

Moms discontent for him wasn't easy to break down, but between Tom and I we finally got her to relax around him. To the point where she would allow us to be alone without having one of my brothers watching us.

Tom dress morally conservative and always called before showing up making sure not to ruin all we accomplished to do. Going to the effort that when he did come over he always brought something for my mother, bothers, and I.

Nothing elaborate but, appealingly generous, and appreciated by mom. Like a vase, or some sort of figurine. That he could refer too that would complement her on her appearance.

Mom was a hard working women, but still an attractive one when she wanted to be, and the more Tom was coming over.

The more attractive she wanted to present herself too him. As well as becoming increasingly more obligingly supportive towards him.

Actually coming out telling him that she believed Helen when she told her that he didn't touch her physically, and was willing to go to court to tell the judge. That she believes her daughter when she said he didn't touch her.

Tom answered all my mother's questions frankly, and even told her that he was a bouncer at a Go-Go bar and had no ill intentions towards Helen. Other than he became very fond of her, and enjoyed the conversations they would have together and just wanted to continue to be friends with her and her family as well.

That at this point in Helen's life she could use a friend, even though the police felt that he wronged her.

That they both knew differently, and he wasn't going to ruin a good friendship because of what anyone thinks about him.

His ever so smooth mannerism worked their magic on mom, but wasn't totally convincing her that he never touched Helen in a physical way, but enough so that she was going to give him the benefit of the doubt.

By believing him when he said that he hired her at first because he felt sorry for her, then became found of her as he became more appreciative of the good job she was doing.

Then when he finally told her mom that he was on the verge of asking the women he's been dating to marry him. While unknown to her that he was referring to Helen when he was saying it rally won her over to his side.

As for Helen's brothers. He would pack them all in his car, and drive them down to the beach, or just kick back with them. When he could find the time to stop over to play some sort of sport, or talk man talk amongst them.

While just stopping by occasionally at first. Until he started showing up on a regular bases having dinner with the family

Even when he was somewhat bruised up several time. From having to kick some drunks out of the bar, or when things got sort of rough and got him tired out from working the irregular hours he was.

It wasn't easy for Tom, and I to get a chance to be alone at first, but as time pasted and ma, became more relaxed, we were getting more and more time to spend together.

Ma, worked days Tom worked night from 9 PM, too past 3 AM in the morning, and I was back in school.

So Tom rented a studio apartment about two blocks from the school where I would skip a day, or two during the week, or leave early to go join him at his place.

It wasn't easy, but Tom was going all out to get me back and too win my mother on his side. While we were both counting the days until I turned eighteen.

Where on one could have any say over the two of us being together, but mean-time I more so than Tom had to be careful. Knowing that I was obviously being watched by the cops.

I would take a change of clothes to school with me.

Wearing them under my clothes so that I could change in the bathroom at school so I could take off to go meet up with Tom at his place.

Taking the back entrance door to get into his apartment building, and using the key he left under his doormat so that I could get into his apartment. Not wanting to risk getting caught carrying it around like I did the last time.

Finding him sleeping most of the time from getting to the apartment later than usual for some reason or another.

DISPLACEMENT INTENT

Getting back before school let out wasn't easy by any means. Tom park his car a block down from his apartment house. Too where I had to learned how to drive on my own. Taking his car, and parking it close to the school.

So that I could sneak back into school and change back into my school clothes so that I could come walking out of the school along with all the other kids.

Just in case I was being watched by the cops Tom bought me a wig to wear when I left the apartment house to disguise myself that I kept hidden in the house, or shoved down in my purse when going to school.

Some days when Tom and I really got carried away with coming together. It gets uncomfortable rough on me to even walk.

That's why he let me drive his car instead of running the risk of him having to drive me, and maybe being seen by the cops.

There were a few days when I convinced ma, that I was sick, and after my brothers left for school. I had Tom come sneaking into the house, where we went upstairs into the antic and spent the whole day together.

I even managed to convinced Tom into buying protection, but he would ever use them. Even though we had one hell of a scare the month before when I miss my friend.

When I said we. I should have said me. Tom was ecstatic when he thought he got me pregnant, and even though I hated to admit. That I was extremely happy myself, but only up to a point. When the thought of having to take care of a child was making a nervous-wrack out of me.

I wanted to be a mother too Tom's children, but I loved being more of a wife, and I didn't want anything to change. Including my body, nor my life by having to tend too, or taking care of kids all over again.

When all I was doing was taking care of my brothers. I wanted to be free to live my life as I wanted to live it.

Meaning not being responsible to anyone, but the man I loved being constantly being made love too who loved m me just the way I was, and becoming a mother would only ruin everything for me.

I was naive but I wasn't stupid. I never stopped noticing the way grown women were looking at him, and I was about to let them give him anything I can't, and better then they could. Knowing that I still had a lot to learn able how to keep him interested in me applying all my time and effort on concentrating on his every whim as well as my own.

It wasn't as if I didn't trust him. I just didn't thrust every other woman, and his willpower to resist the temptations they will definitely be placing before him. I wanted him to be totally blinded by wanting me only.

As things worked out. It was a false alarm, and was I ever relieved, but yet there I went letting him having his way, and loving every illustriously second of it. Ignorantly hoping, and praying that he wasn't going to get me pregnant.

Both Tom and I wanted to make sure that we keep things out in the open where my family was concern.

Where I made it a point to empathize on the fact that after I turned 18 that Tom and I were thinking about becoming more than just friends.

Preparing my mother that things were changing between the two, of us to the point where were might even start dating.

Where my mother didn't like that idea one bit, but I couldn't help to notice her developing a fondness towards Tom that she was becoming increasingly more affected that was becoming exceedingly more than just likeness.

By the way she was dressing herself, and the way she was warming up to him getting closer and closer to him, and was even finding excuses of hugging herself up against him. Making sure to compress her breasts and pelvic region firmly against him.

I had to stop her from developing any sexual attachment towards him before she might come in between Tom and I.

Like I said before my mother was still an attractive woman. Who hasn't been involved with a man for a long time, that I knew of.

Even though she's had several male friends. She never made it obvious that there was anything sexual going on between them.

Where she sure was warming up to Tom. By wearing low cut blouses, and skin tight skirts, and tight shorts.

Even though she was trying to be discreet about her attentions to us kids. She sure was making herself extremely available for Tom to make advance towards her.

DISPLACEMENT INTENT

By stimulatingly enticing him to approach her with the intent of wanting to become more than just friends.

Tom and I discus my suspicions several time, and even though he assured me than he wasn't interested in my mothers. I still was having a hard time believing that he was telling me the truth.

Being jealous of one's own mother might seem very petty, and that she made me feel insecure of my ability of being able to maintain Tom's interest, but I was honestly actually finding myself competing with my own mother for the man I loved.

That's when I for the first in my life realized that I could never be ignorant about ever trusting any other women to be alone with Tom.

When I saw with my own eyes my own mother thinking that she could be more of a woman to him that I could be.

I saw other girl competing against each other over guys, and never realized too what extent they might have to resort too, to retain his interest in her.

Where I didn't go through all I did to have some other women take him away from me. I never thought that I could be vindictive against my own mothers.

Hatful, and spiteful yes, but never vindictively spiteful against her. To where I would actually look upon her as a rival against me, and the thought frightened the hell out of me. That she might be able to seduce him into having sex with her, more than having sex with me.

My suspicions didn't become a threatening reality until the day she asks Tom to help her with her car out in the garage, and she lead him out of the kitchen door taking hold of his hand to see if he could help her.

Ma, was wearing a low cut blouse and no bra, and an extra tight shorts really showing her ass off to him along with her pelvic area compress underneath those shots.

As my brothers and I remained inside watching TV. When suddenly it dawned on me that ma, and Tom have been gone for some time, So I went out to check on what was going on.

That's when I saw ma, leaning over one of the car fenders across from Tom with her breasts practically fully exposed draping beneath her blouse.

Not hindering him from letting him get an eyeful of them as I walked up asking, how things were going.

That's when I knew that my mother was going after the man I loved, and I wasn't going to let her get away with it if I had anything to do about it, but I couldn't do anything that would disrupt all are hard work to get my mother on Tom's and my side.

So I had no choice but to overlook what I saw, and turn an ignorantly blind eye. Too stand between them at the front of the car.

Then to inadvertently draw attention to my mother's appearance saying.

"Ma, shouldn't you go put a sweater on it's starting to get somewhat chilly out."

Luckily there were only a few more weeks before Tom had to appear in court, and all I really had to content with was weekends, or when might get a night off work to keep getting in between them. While making sure to let Tom know how I felt about what my own mother was trying to do.

Where he just laughed my concerns off saying." Come on honey there's no way you mother could stand a chance against you.

Sure I looked I'm only human, but why would I settle for just looking when I can hold far more beautiful breasts... relax I'll have you out once we get through this.

I'm a big boy now.

I see naked breasts every night at the club, and I know when I'm privileged to be the sole possessor of the most lavishing breast of all time. Beside it's going to take a lot more than breasts too ever get me to betray my love for you.

This world is full of beautiful women on the outside, but on the inside there's none more stupendously ravishing divine than you."

What could I do, but to believe him when he was right about seeing women breasts, and I had to admit that I was putting too much emphasis on him becoming sexually interested in my mothers, and I vainly believed in what he said about me being divine in every respect.

DISPLACEMENT INTENT

✳ ✳ ✳ ✳

It wasn't until I finally got to meet his attorney Phil during the finally few weeks before Tom's trial was to come up that I vainly confirmed Tom's definition about my splendor.

That guy was as sly as a fox, and as slippery, and sneaker than a greased pig.

He knew his business and even coached me as how to act, and conduct myself while in the courtroom.

While at the same time drawing my attention on how he was concentrating on not taking his eyes off me. His eyes heat was so intensely violating me. They made me feel as if they were striping me naked groping me making me feel extremely nervous around him.

Even as I clung to tom's arm openly expressing Tom was the man I was in love with, which he blatantly ignored and kept violating me with those burning eyes of his.

Ma, was still sort of sitting on the fence where Tom was concerned. Mainly because I got the feeling that she was harboring personal feelings towards Tom herself, and was sort of jealous of us getting so close to each other. Using the age difference between us not to justify the relationship.

Then just before the day Tom was supposed to appear in court. He bought me a blue sweater outfit. That he said he wanted me to wear when I went into the courtroom with him.

The second I but it on. I knew what he was up to. The outfit clung to me like a second skin accentuating my exquisite body features.

Empathizing on the fullness of my breasts alone with the prestigious curvatures of every illustrious inch of my body.

He even went as far as asking me not to wear a bra, or even panties. Knowing that my pelvic region was sure to bulge out, and my breasts nipples would perturb out beneath the clinging material of the conforming sweater.

When it came to the next day Tom proudly walked me into the courtroom all decked out the way he wanted me to appear.

Instantly getting everyone eyes sitting in the courtroom to startlingly ogle me, and the way the outfit clung to my body. Using it to immediately insight a four-drawn conclusion to everyone in the courtroom. Especially the male patience that there would be no way I could be a virtuous teenage girl of 17.

Causing me to become the focus of everyone attention including even the judges. Even I felt that I was looking ravishingly gorgeous, and couldn't help to flaunt my exquisiteness.

Sashaying my naked butt beneath the constricting skirt that the sun's rays were provocatively peering through. Making sure to intensifying attract the full attention of everyone in the courtroom.

As Tom proudly paraded me walking down the center aisle to seated me in the front role for the judge not to be able to take his ogling eyes off my braless breasts. Before going to join his attorney.

The second I saw Tom's attorney's eyes even ogling me with lustful wanting desire in his transfixed eyes I know that it was Tom's attorney Phil who put him up to parading me down the aisle before everyone in that courtroom.

Then when he stood up, and ask me to stand before the judge with my long satiny smooth red hair covering my head accentuating my gorgeous face.

Whose eyes were already extensively locked onto my enticing breasts protruding nipples. Too where Tom's attorney had to speak up more than twice to get the judges attention on him so he could ask.

"Your honor does she look seventeen, years old to you?"

The case against Tom was dismissed due to the fact that I lied about my age. Some 20 minutes into the trail.

When Tom, my mother, and I left the courthouse together. Walking behind two very angry detectives who lost their case against Tom, and went storming out of the courtroom.

A week later I moved into Tom's apartment without my mother's blessings, but with her consent. To which baffled me knowing the attachment she was forming towards him, and her knowing what us was going to transpire between the two, of us sexually.

It wasn't like her to accept us having sex together and knowingly condone it. Something wasn't right, and I knew it, but I wasn't about to go making trouble for myself by pushing her to tell me why. Not when I was getting my way and having Tom all for myself legally as well.

Mom would even drop over to visit on occasions along with my brothers who were really hitting it off with Tom.

What I was finding even more puzzling was the fact that we were sort of becoming a happy family group at long last, but not so happy that I ever let up suspecting my mother too be up to no good. She was up to something and I damn well knew it.

It was that glowing look about her that was getting to me, but I never caught onto what she was conniving in that devious mind of hers.

* * *

Things were going great for us. Tom was even trying to go straight. With the exception of having to deal with a few urgent calls that he had to attend too.

He even quit his job as the bounce, and started working for an Awing company hanging canvas awnings.

The money wasn't all that great, but it was an honest job, and we didn't have to struggle all that much.

Tom had a small fortune stashed away for us to fall back on, but it was obviously beginning to show that Tom was starting to miss his old way of life.

Mainly by him becoming increasingly more restless while having to hang around the house doing nothing, but sitting watching TV, and no being able to go out and spend frivolously wine and dine me, or buying me trinkets.

It was getting so that he wasn't even venturing into his other apartment to work out as strenuously as he once did.

As the days relentlessly continued to seem like years before I would be turning eighteen, and my age would no longer be a threat of separating us. Eight, months pasted Helen turn eighteen, Helen now eighteen, Tom twenty-three

* * * *

Eight, mouths after I first meet Tom we were married and a mouth later Tom became a hunted man.

The police came to the apartment looking for Tom saying that he was involved in an attempted hi-jacking of a mink truck in Iowa. Where a shooting took place, and all but one of the Hijackers were shot and killed. Saying that they suspected that the one who got away was Tom. Them they preceded to question me asking me where he was.

All I could say was that he was out, and that it couldn't had been him because he's been home with me for the past five, days.

That he's been sick, and he was out looking for a job because his employer fired him because he couldn't come into work.

I gave the police Tom's employers name, and the address where he once worked. Knowing that Tom was fired because I called his boss each day calling him in sick like he told me too.

After they left I called Carol at the Tike Club. She told me that she heard about what happened, but hasn't heard from Tom. That if she does she would contact me right away.

That night I staged a fake argument to make the neighbors think that Tom was home, and went storming out of the apartment. There-by assuring that Tom would have an alibi, and a reason for not being at home if the cops came back.

I couldn't contact Tom's lawyer until I was sure he was alright. Money was no problem. Tom and I opened a joint checking account, and Tom made me aware of the locations of other places where I could obtain money if I needed it, and we always kept a couple of thousand dollars hidden in the other apartment for emergencies.

Even though the five-day limit pasted I still refused to leave and go home to my mother. Something kept telling me that Tom might be alright and that he was still alive, and would make his way back to me, and I wasn't going to give up hope that I was right.

Two weeks past. Then on a Friday morning around 9 AM, the phone rang. I nervously answered it not knowing want to expect to hear on the end. When

DISPLACEMENT INTENT

I nearly had a heart attack right there, and then as I heard Tom's voice saying.

"Helen honey it's me Tom. Now don't say a word just listen. I'm alright, but I'm in Chicago...

I want you to get on the train and met me at the central train station. I'll be there from the hours of 1 PM, too 3 PM each day.

When you leave. Tell no one where you are going, and make it look like that you were just going out shopping.

When you get there, go sit by the magazine stand and I'll come to you. Honey I'm alright just get here..." He hung up saying.

I didn't stop to think. I just gathered up a few things and shoved everything into one of my large handbags, and grabbed up what cash I had in the apartment then picked up my purse and coat, and went out the door.

Hailing a cab while attempting to walk calmly in the direction to the train station, and took it down to the train station.

I bought a ticket and boarded the first train heading to Chicago and boarding it at 10:45 that evening, and got off it at 2 AM in the morning of the next day, and took another cab to the closest hotel some three, blocks away from the station.

Where I sat up impatiently watching the clock to noon, and left too hail another cab to take me to central train station. That was about a mile away from the hotel. Too do what Tom told me to do.

Getting there about 12:30. Where I sat for nearly two, long nerve-racking hours impatiently waiting for him too show up. Before I spotted him emerging from a telephone booth, skeptically looking around.

Ecstatically I jerked up, and ran up to him, and into his waiting loving arms. Making a spectacle out of myself.

Frantically hugging, and kissing him while crying tears of anguishing joy. Wanting to reach up and ring his damn neck.

Only to discover that when I put too much of my weight against him, that he would jolt back grunting out in pain. Using the telephone booth to brace himself up, grabbing for his left leg.

"My god…!" I panicky asked! Not being able to control my concern for what caused him so much pain.

" What happen to you…?! Are you alright…" I nervously asked. While aiding him to stand up using my bodies weigh to hold him against the telephone boot.

"I got shot in the leg… It hurts like hell but it was taking care of by a doctor I knew… Now come on we can't stand around here drawing attention to ourselves."

He took my arm saying, stepping out away from the phone booth. Using me to brace himself up as he walked with a very distinguishable limp to his left side, as we walked towards the main door leaving the station.

I hailed a cab, and took it back to my hotel where I was already registered in. Where we spent the rest of the day and night holding up, where I helped him take care of his leg.

The bullet took a large chunk out of the side of his thigh that someone stitched up damn good, but was going to be leaving one hell of a scar.

Lying in bed together he was attempting to avoid telling how he got himself shot by trying to get me to make love to him.

Instead of telling me what happen, but the pain to his legs was unbearable. Any movement on the mattress would inflict immediate pain to his leg.

I was so ecstatically happy that he was alive, nothing else mattered. I was so grateful just to be lying next to him, and it was frustrating the hell out of me that I couldn't show him how much I missed and loved him. Without inflicting a lot of pain and discomfort on him.

Needless to say, thanks to Tom's creativeness I found a way to make us both very happy to be back together again by allowing myself to be persuaded to patronize him.

* * * *

Afterwards I laid resting my head resting upon his chest telling him what happened at the apartment, and what I did to give him an alibi.

Empathizing on how I was beside myself with grief worrying about him. Not knowing if he was alive, or lying dead someplace.

DISPLACEMENT INTENT

Telling him that I just couldn't give up on him never coming back to me to go running back home after five days. Knowing in my heart that he was still alive.

Bringing up the fact that the cops said everyone was killed, and it appeared that only one person got away, and how they felt sure it was him.

Tom was noticing just how upset I was and having extreme trouble calming myself down and start to massage my neck letting his magic finger work their magic.

After calming me down somewhat. He them preceded to tell me his version of what happen. Starting out with saying right off." It was a set-up... They were waiting for us to hit that truck."

He then told me what he had to do after escaping the fire fight. How he had to crawl, and sleep in swearers for days. Making his way to this doctor he knew to get patched up.

Which I find out to be an outright lie sometime later, but at the time. As far as I was concern it was over, and Tom was alive and safe.

I didn't care about anything or anyone else. All I cared about was we were back together, and our lives would return back to moral once I got him back home.

"Honey believe me I'm sorry, but I had to do it for us. It was to be my last job. After it was over my boss was going to let me walk away...

I'm out of it now Helen. For good I'm out of it. I've his word on it... I just had to do it for us honey."

He pleadingly kept saying trying to console my concerns of having repercussion over what happened.

Knowingly ling to me. Knowing differently that there was no getting out for him, not with all he knew about who was who, and everything that was going on.

That could incriminate so many influential people, but he wasn't about to tell me what he really suspected.

That him even thinking of getting out was like him signing his own death warrant. That no one walks away, and he wasn't going to be any different.

From the age of ten, when Tom was adopted into the syndicate by one of the head kingpins. He was groomed extensively orientated into the organization solely for one purpose by his adopted benefactor. Trained to be his adopted fathers number one contact and bodyguard within his organization.

Figure heads in the syndicate evolved since the gangster era. They learned that knowledge was not only power, but the means of their survival.

That the more one could obtain. Not only against another figure head, but also about prominent influential effluent members that were involved in the operation of the city's business. The longer they would continue to live, prosper, and avoid being arrested, and sent to prison.

That's where Tom came in and became so knowledgeable. That only one person knew of his potential beside his benefactor.

Tom was his benefactor's adopters secret who was conditioned to become the keeper of all his adopted father's secrets.

He was the one in the possession of the locations, places and names of documentation could be obtained that could be used against his fellow head syndicate figures.

That if anything happened to him those secret was to be sent to the people who could use the information against his associate figure heads within the organization, or to be used as proof to convict those who allow the syndicate to operate outside the law.

In the event if anything unexpected should befall him, like being killed unexpectedly regardless whether it was by someone in the organization, or not

Tom was trained on how to stay alive while he moved about within the syndicate organization. While acting as his adopted father's official bodyguard, or executioner.

Which isolating him from having to become involved with the thuggery that went on by the thugs and soldiers in the lower levels of the organization.

This adopted father was one of a few who had the foresight to insure his future within the organization. By having the ability to be able to prove anything he authoritatively presented against another figure head within the organization to insure his wellbeing, and longevity.

If it was ever discovering that Tom was the one in possession of such evidence, and it's whereabouts.

His life wouldn't be worth a dime after they got what they wanted to know out of his adopted father as well as him.

In essence it was the syndicate itself who was insuring his welfare. As he went about carrying out his obligations with the organization just like anyone else so that he would blend in and not appear any more special than anyone else who was one of the boss's bodyguard.

While his main purpose was to maintain, and obtain information from the sources provided to him solely for his adopted father when called upon to do so and supply it to the persons or person directed to receive it.

While Tom was out following orders he was going about totally undetected within the organization secretly locating others like him so he could earn their trust and confidence until he found out what the other person was being entrusted with.

Then obtain it without having to eliminate the person entrusted with it if at all necessary not to do so. So that it wouldn't be discovered that it was discovered.

Tom should have known better to even think that he would be an exception. When he alone was sent out to eliminate those with by far more power, and influence than himself. Never really knowing the content of the information he was collecting and holding the locations of.

The syndicate doesn't care how much they spend on anyone. Nor did Tom know if he was the only one harboring secrets.

Thereby not knowing who he himself could trust only doing what he was told and don't ask question, or say anything about anything he knew about.

It was what one might know and trying to walk away with that concerns them, and Tom knew too much to be trusted not to say anything.

The only reason that anyone within the syndicate would dare put Tom in harm's way. Would be because someone was thinking to eliminate his benefactor, and thought that Tom could be the one that was holding all the secrets.

Then set it up to look as if I was killed doing a job. To not set off any alarms towards his benefactors, and his welfare, or he as well as his entire family where going to suffer the same fate he was going to suffer along with those who were loyal to him.

What I came to find out, and what horrified me even more. As far as I concern. I was as good as dead if it was known for sure that Tom was officially dead. That I would soon to be also dead.

That I had no means of retaliating, or to stop them from killing me. That Tom wasn't about to tell me either when I married him.

That I was virtually stuck in the life I chose for myself. That was one of the reasons why he took me out to show me off amongst his friends.

Because he was obligated to do as all the others were also obligated to do. When they became involved with some women, or got married just in case they broke up, or they felt they could put something over on anyone within the organization.

Which Tom overlooked telling me when he was out showing me off. Was he being in fact setting me up to be killed if I dared to leave him, or if I would kill him personally myself if I ever found out what he was doing to me.

"Tom are you telling me the truth... Is it really over...?"

"Yes, honey it's over... Well sort of...?" He skeptically insinuated." Honey being over doesn't mean that it's over. I just have to be extremely careful. I did make a lot of enemies over the years, but yes, overall.

I'm out of it for the time being, at least until after all this settles down. I still might have to continue to do what they tell me, but after they find out that it was a setup.

I'm sure they're going to have me keep a low profile. We'll worry about that if, and when the time comes.

As for us making it. If I've to scrub floors, we'll make it. If I can't support you I don't deserve you. Now don't you think we should get some sleep before we start heading back home tomorrow?"

"I'm not tired. For some reason I'm all wound up. I need something to take my mind off all this bull-shit." I rolled over on my side turning my back towards Tom no longer looking up into Tom's face speaking out."

Harboring an uneasy feeling that Tom was not only being evasive, but also ling to me. That he was harboring something going on in the back of his mind, and that what happened to him was far from over where he was concern.

Noticing that each time he mentions "That it was an it was a setup "That he instantly became extremely tensed up, and upset to the point where he would get extremely distant. As if contemplating something over in his mind.

Giving me the impression knowing Tom the way I did. That he was contemplating taking revenge on those he might think betrayed him, and who nearly got him killed in the process.

CHAPTER 5

The next morning, we bought train tickets heading back home. As far as I was concern Tom was safe, and we were back together again, and that was all that mattered.

What I didn't count on was the law still being interested in him after I established an alibi to his whereabouts during the time they were trying to implicate him elsewhere.

Even though Tom had himself an alibi me. The police still came and arrested him and charged him with complicity in a hi-jacking.

They even had the nerve to offer Tom the opportunity to cop a plea bargain if he would talk, and tell them what went down, and who was behind the hijacking. Of course he didn't take it. He was that dedicated to the syndicate.

During the next year Tom was totally ignored by the syndicate, and most of his money went to pay attorney fees to postpone expedition back to Iowa. As he fought his case of false arrest in Milwaukee.

Finally winning, and all charges were dropped from Iowa. During which Tom went back to work working for the same awing company where he got fired from. Where his ex-boss called him and even gave him a rise if he would come back to work for him.

Tom was subsequently on his own, and supposedly out of the syndicate, while still constantly being hassled by the police.

Just barging in our apartment any time they wanted. Every time when something happened in the neighborhood where we lived.

However, he was still associating with Carol the proprietor of the Tike Club, helping out when he could. Who was unknowingly a go between the syndicate and Tom.

During which Tom wasn't making all that much money, and she would subsidize us helping us paying the bills.

During which I became familiar of my circumstances regarding my position of being Tom's wife. With Carol constantly telling me, that I should be grateful that Tom was so well appreciated, and trusted within the syndicate.

That the syndicate didn't usually cater to anyone who was able to divulge information of the organization business, by allowing them to live through all we have being living through.

That I should be honored that Tom is held in such high esteem.

That's when she warned me to never give the organization any excuse to think that neither of us can't be trusted. If I wanted to continue to live.

Carol was deeply involved with the syndicate, and during her comings and goings we became really close friends.

Carol was an extremely gorgeous woman, however at least five, years older that Tom was, and even though it was obvious that there was something between Tom and her that they were sharing between themselves. I felt sure I had nothing to worry about where her and Tom were concern.

I never could connect what it was that made them so responsible towards each other. Even though they never hindered themselves to hide the dictation they sheared towards each other by the way they would respond to each other's physical gestures, or the other amorous impulsiveness when it came to pushing, shoving and even groping each other.

Even though I came to discover that the two, of them were intimately involved off and on during their relationship and established an unbreakable bond between themselves.

Even though they both displayed their susceptibleness for them to have everyone thing there was something going on between them.

They both made a concentrated effort not to become emotionally involved with each other, and it wasn't from out of mutual respect for me, or my marriage to Tom.

Tom was a one women man in every respect, and Carol not only respected him for it. She made it a point to support me in assuring that he didn't break his vow he made to me.

I was the first to admit their relationship was an uncanny one, but I always figured that there was something going on between the two of them.

That only they knew about that cause them to tolerate each other's position. Regardless in the manner in which they express themselves.

Carol had one hell of a temper, and wasn't apprehensive about the way she would express herself even when the two, of them got into a heated disagreement when things would get physical. As well as for when they compromised and made up.

I honestly believed when Tom said he wasn't physically involved with Carol. Even though it sounded, and appeared too incredible to be believed I ignorantly took it for granted.

On the scale from one, though ten, Carol was no less than a twenty.

Any guy would kill just to be seen with her. Let along become romantically involved with her, and Tom could never say no, to her when she as a favor of him, and the same went for her where he was concern.

Without my knowledge Tom was busted for soliciting for some of Carol's girls. Carol was running a call girl service through the club using the topless dancers.

Carol was having trouble financially. A lot of people who were regulars at her place were having legal problems of their own, and she had to cut prices, and cut back on her staff.

As well as branch out with the services she was offering due to the fact that business as usual was having to reduce her income drastically.

She went to Tom too asked him to help her with the prostitution business she was running on the side.

Seeing how she was already using him to protect them if a client got out of control, or if they attempted to ditch out without paying. She would even use him to go pick of the women if they called, and ask him too.

Carol was never known for taking responsibility for any she became involved with, or was running for herself, or for the syndicate. She always had someone else handling that end of things for her, and I that's where Tom came in and was expected to handle for her.

Seeing how she was being protected by several figure head of the syndicate that actually owned the club she was running.

She was not only provocatively sexy, she was very demanding, and got her way even amongst the highly fear criminal leaders operating in the city.

One didn't cross her and get away with it, and if she asks for something she morally got what she ask for.

Helen didn't come to find out until after Tom was arrested. That Tom knew Carol since he was a young boy of ten, and knew actually like she was like. That she wasn't anything like she made herself appear to be like. That she was even more cold heated than he was, and twice as unscrupulously diabolical in nature.

He knew first hand just how unmerciful and deadly she could be if she was forced to revert back to her old self.

That was unknown too everyone who knew her with the exception of Tom and only a few others within the syndicate.

Even though she was five years older than Tom. Their feeling towards each other remained uncanny to say the least. seeing how Tom was married, but everyone kept their opinions to themselves. Not wanting to get themselves involved in other people's business.

Time were hard for everyone, and Tom was just trying to help her out doing her a favor on the side without telling me, because of what she was doing for us.

The cops were cracking down hard on prostitution. Tom spent the last of our money on bailing Carol out, and to show her appreciation Carol took off until things cooled off.

Not letting anyone know where she was going. Leaving Tom and I holding the bag for the rest of her bail money.

Which we couldn't afford to foot the bill for, but never the less we were stuck with it, and if that wasn't bad enough.

Those damn cops never stopped harassing us. They were out to make our life as difficult as they could, and they were getting away with it.

Just hoping that Tom would make a mistake so they could throw the book at him, and put him behind bars. Too join all his friends who lived long enough to be sent to prison.

Over a year pasted since Tom and I were married the cops still wouldn't let us alone. They were still continuing to come banging on our door at all hours of the day and night.

Hoping to catch Tom not at home. Asking to come in to have a look around the apartment. Saying that they're just investigating a shooting, or a burglary, or a mugging in the area answering to his description

Tom would tell them to get lost, but they still kept coming back, and we couldn't afford paying any attorney to file a harassment law suit against the police department.

It was just damn luck that Tom was home, and not out earning some extra money doing what he did best on the side, but it was only going to be a matter of time before they found something to pin on Tom so that they could arrest him.

During all this time the cops never found out about Tom's secret apartment across the hall. Where Tom would relentlessly go work out to practice his martial arts, keeping his hand battered, and bruised up.

Purposely in order to cover up what he was really using them for when he went out earning us some extra money collecting on a commission bases from deadbeats who weren't paying what they owed.

So that if he was every questioned he would have an excuse for why his hands were always battered and cut up.

Making sure to keep his membership active in one of his cohort Duo giving himself an iron clad alibi.

Working for friends he kept in contact with, but having to take only half the commission he would normally charge. Too keep everyone from finding out that he was working again.

I had to admit the money did help relieve a lot of the frustration that was building up between Tom and I, but having Tom suppress himself was taking a toll on him.

Provoking Tom the way they were doing and that it wasn't in Tom's nature too let anyone push him around the way the cops were doing wasn't something Tom was being able to tolerate without having a rebellious effect on him.

DISPLACEMENT INTENT

Our sex life wasn't compensating for all the stressful aggravation the cops were inflicting on our married life, and the pressure was getting to both of us.

Sex was only acting only as a temporary sensitive. Aggravating are situation even that much more at times.

It took everything I could use to prevent him from getting back at those cops, and believe me if I wouldn't have turned the other cheek so to say constantly pleading with him saying.

"Honey we've gone this far to give up now. Please don't do anything foolish to destroy all that we have been struggling for. Trust me honey if you do something now I'll never forgive you... I swear...!"

Those cop would have been kissing his ass to avoid having to go home to an empty house, or one filled with chaos, or fear for what might happen to their wives, and families.

There were very few people Tom would let over rule his intent to revenge himself, and those cops weren't any different, and it took everything I had and more to keep him suppressed from carrying out his aggressive nature.

The longer I lived with Tom the more I horrifically discovered about him and the loving, kind heated, and gentle person I married.

Although I personally never felt threatened by him

I couldn't help to feel nothing but pity for those who were unfortunate to comfort him unknowing that they were coming face to face with the devil's advocate himself.

Tom took great pride in knowing all about how to be sadistic and unscrupulous in nature. He wouldn't have and conscious, or second thoughts about paying secret visits to their families, and do more than set the fear of God, into any of them.

Where it wouldn't matter to him what sex they were, or how old. To insure that they would become more that terrified of him ever coming back.

Tom constrain was wearing thin along with my own to not let him loose once and for all. What those cops were doing was effecting my life drastically. Personally, emotionally, as well as physically, and it was beginning to take its toll on me by making a nervous-racket out of me.

Tom told me a story about a friend of his. When he was but a teenager himself about his friend Bill who the cops were always harassing.

His friend had this girlfriend that the cops would always harasses every chance they could and kept saying to her. "Tell us want we want to hear and we'll stop."

My friend Bill finally had enough and went out seeking those two cops out. The first one who he despised the most. He went after his and wife and two kids. Not in the typical way by attacking them first, and working his way up to him.

He told me that his friend Bill went after the cops first. To attack him on his job by using a very close friend of his. To set this particular cop up good, and not in the moral way.

His friend was a mortician, and Bill wanted to make sure that cops would never bother him again.

Bill waited for the cop's family to leave the house as usual. With his wife driving her kids to school. Making sure she had an accident on the way to keep her away from the house for a few hours.

Bill had his friend bring a cadaver in and placed her made up naked body on their bed, and had his friend dress up like the cop holding a gun in his hand.

Knowing that this particular cop wouldn't be at work, but with his mistress that he was having a secret affair with from his wife.

His friend stood made up to look like this cop sideways beside the bed where the body was lying naked in his own bedroom and had his friend fired three, shoots into her while he took multiple pictures.

Making sure that what they filled her with that looked like blood would spatter about the sheets. Then they gathered up everything and left.

Several days later this cops received an envelope with the pictures showing him holding the smoking gun.

Killing some young naked girl in his own bedroom making sure to show the sheets and pillows. Along with a note, and a peace of the bloody sheet attacked inside saying.

"Your hassling days are over. One more time and these picture will be sent to your boss and the DA where it will be for you to prove that you didn't kill her.

DISPLACEMENT INTENT

If that doesn't stop, you more will be sent to your wife along with the address of the other woman you've been sleeping with.

Fuck with me or any of my friends again, and maybe the next time the women lying on the bed will be who knows. Maybe someone closest to your partner. Just to let him know what sort of person you really are." (Murderer)!!!

Tom went on to say. That it appears that the same thing happened to his partner, but his sec partner was even closer than a wife. Like his sister."

It wasn't like Tom to be that sinister. Tom would have must likely attacked him when the cop was least expecting it, and mash his head in with a lead pile, and leave the cop brain dead, or crippled for life just for spite, or to use as an example.

Now that's was Tom. He was all that considerate, or conniving when it comes to reaping revenge. Tom wouldn't stoop that low to be patient enough to be so manipulative about destroying someone, especially a cops no less.

I knew when he told me that story who Bill was. Even though I felt certain that wasn't the Tom I knew under the same circumstances. I also had no doubt in my mind once I stopped to think about what he said.

Knowing Tom, the way I did it suddenly dawned on me what Tom was trying to do. Was his way of asking me for my permission to follow his friends example, and I was damn close to saying.

" You know I wouldn't, or couldn't blame him for what he did. Someone had to teach those cops a lesson that they would never forget" But, I couldn't allow myself to say it.

So I ignored commenting on his tall tale, and refused to acknowledge that his tale made any sense, and distracted him by taking his mind off his friend Bill and back on me.

Afterwards I went back to continue to endure, and endure, and endure the harassment until I felt sure that Tom wasn't going to wait any longer for my permission. When by some miracle something miraculous happen to change everything. Including our lives as well.

CHAPTER 6

Tom was looking in the want ads for a new, and better job and spotted a job opening that said. (Trainee Machinist wanted to work at large industrial plant in California.)

"Helen honey." Tom enthusiastically spoke out getting my attention wanting to show me the advertisement excitedly speaking out.

"Honey it's a chance at a new life for ourselves, but I don't know the first thing about being a machinist?"

My words were." No one ever did when they first started. Let's answer the advertisement and go find out about it before we get to excited over it."

Tom went for the interview, and too both are disbelief, he actually got hired. However, there was one hitch to actually getting the position.

Tom had to be on the job site within sixty, days, and he had to pay his own way there in order to be reimbursed, and to get the sum of $1,000 when he arrived that was agreed he would be paid.

Too which we didn't have a cent to are name. We had nothing as it was, and was living in a furnished antic apartment. Living form pay check to pay check where he was only making $5.00 per hour, but that wasn't going to stop Tom.

He saw the opportunity of a lifetime, and he was determined to go for it. Even knowing that he lied on the application to get the job, and knowing the consequences behind him just up and taking off without telling anyone where he was going. Especially the syndicate, knowing what would happen if they ever found out where he was at.

Tom hit on a scheme to get the money we needed. What we need was a car first and foremost, and at least a thousand bucks. Along with a new driver's license giving himself a new identity.

Even though he made a mistake when filling out the job application using his real name, and social security number.

DISPLACEMENT INTENT

His thought was too establishing two, identities one, for work, and the other to hide himself from anyone who was going to be looking for him.

I had to admit. It was an ingenious plan. He would rent an unfurnished apartment. Then would go out, and finance the furniture too fill it using his real name and work history.

Then sell the furniture to buy the car, and get most of the money he financed for the furniture back by selling it as well.

Then just before we would leave he would cash checks to get even more money for us to live on until we got to California. Before we left the state.

All we had to do was to open another checking account, and go overdrawn. Telling me that there's nothing illegal about not having sufficient funds. Which would give us a good week or more before the checks would start to bounce.

His idea worked within 6 weeks we were driving out of Milwaukee with some $4,500 in cash with six, weeks to spare with only what we could shove into the trunk of the car. Heading for are new life in California leaving are old miscible life behind us.

Both knowing the risk. With Tom making sure that he was the one doing all the signing, selling, and crashing the checks.

Knowing that he would be the one to be arrested not I, if the cops ever caught up to him as the one cashing the checks while leaving Milwaukee.

Where he tossed the check books away leaving no trail for anyone to follow or find out in which direction we headed. Driving with a new driver's license, and name not telling me how he managed to obtain them.

Making sure that I would be free from going to any jail and continue to live my life without becoming involved in anything he himself did.

Telling me to hold onto $500.00 so that I could make it back home to my family if thing went bad for us out of state. While making sure to keep my madam name out of everything that the cops could possibly prosecute me for so I could use it to make my way back home without being implicated in what he did.

It was shroud of him the way he was going about covering my ass. Once he explained about the furniture. That he bought and sold that wasn't paid for in his name while never mentioning that he was married when he financed everything in his name.

Telling me how the finance company couldn't do anything until he defaulted on the loan, and really couldn't do anything to him, but come and repossess the furniture from the people he sold it all too. Leaving it up to the loan company to locate who they were.

Knowing all the time that it would be the people he sold the furniture to that were going to take the loss, and maybe go to jail for buying stolen property.

He said that everything they did was a misdemeanor, and not eligible for expedition seeing it wasn't a felony crime or one in the state we were heading, and that he never made a=out check for over $100.00 and had that much in his checking account at the time.

Tom knew how to manipulate the law. What he was most concern about was the syndicate finding him and by creating three, different identities he would be making it virtually impossible for anyone to find him while being legal with the company he was going to be working for.

Where he would even make it possible for him to paid taxes to avoid getting involved with the federal government.

Tom even covered his ass from the military. To which he was obligated to serve on a reserve bases by moving over fifty, miles out of range from his home base.

Actually having his company commander sign his release from duty waver. By telling his commander that he had to leave the area to tend to his mother.

What would make it impossible for him to attend his scheduled meeting on a regular basis because she was dying from cancer.

The six, weeks we spent getting to California we made into our honeymoon spending it seeing the country as we drove from state to state.

Living in rented motel rooms to rest and cleaned up in. While having ourselves a ball getting it on in different states as we crossed the county consummating our marriage

DISPLACEMENT INTENT

* * * *

Finally arriving in San Diego California down to are last hundred bucks. Where we stopped at Tom's new place of employment.

Tom went to report in while I waited out in the car for him to come out. Where it took him over an hour before I spotted him coming out.

Waving something in his hand above his head. Which amounted to making us $500.00 richer, along with his new job.

We went out to celebrate. Where while we were eating he explained to me why he only got $500.00, Saying that it had to last until he got his first paycheck in two more weeks.

Tom was furious over how they lied to him.

Leaving him with the impression that he had to work thirty, days on a probationary basis to see if he qualified for the job before he got the other $500.00 that was supposed to have been our expense money that we had to spend to make to the new job.

Tom never counted on us having to find ourselves a place to live, and having to spend the money they gave them to live on. He was counting on the full thousand dollars to do that. That now only amounted to around $600.00. Which had to last us for almost three, weeks including what we had in their pockets.

We were here, and there wasn't anything we could do about the situation. I became so good with money I got so I could squeeze a nickel out of a penny, and we still had some money in our pockets left when Tom finally got his first check.

* * * *

Tom was to start work that next Monday. He didn't have any tools or the vaguest idea what he needed, or how to even start a damn machine.

Tom lied though his teeth to the person he talked to. Saying that he was having his tools shipped by train and that he graduated from high school, and he had a year's training running a drill press, and that he knew how to read gaging instruments. Like micrometers and calipers.

Figuring that he wouldn't last too long, but hopefully long enough for him to obtain the skills of the trade to find another job elsewhere.

He wasn't going to let the lack of not having the skill in need to know stand in his way. All he needed was the chance to learn.

I felt sure that once Tom got his mind set to doing something he would do it. Tom might not have had an education, but he wasn't stupid by any means. I never seen him so determined to make a new life for the both of us.

To talk to him one would think he had a college degree in everything. He even amazed me when I found out that he was actually a mathematic wizard, and had the vocabulary of an English teacher.

Where I got as far as the eleventh grade, and he considered me smart because I knew how to spell. Where I wasn't nearly as intelligent as he was.

He placed me on a pedestal above him where he even made me the financial manager of the household. Knowing the only reason, I was stuck having to be so, was because Tom was as irresponsible as hell when it came to money.

Money never meant anything of important to him, because he always found a way to get more than he needed. So he never concerned himself about spending it.

Where I had to make all the decisions and control all the money. Give it to Tom, and he would be out spending it on showing how damn proud he was showing me off in elegant night spots, or buying me expensive clothes and jewelry.

That man had exquisite taste as well as a provocative one. Like buying cashmere sweaters and silky risqué scanty outfits, along with satin and silk blouses, and silk lined bras not to mention very exotic underwear.

His extravagance never was limited by money when it come to me. His love for me was that precious... No women could have been so anointed with so much prestige.

Where I was frightening as hell, and I couldn't show it, or the fear that I would hurt his feelings. To a guy like Tom where I was the only person who ever mattered to him.

Any form of rejection on my part would affect him drastically. That's how unemotionally unstable he was where I was concern.

The women in California were gorgeous, seductive and easily obtainable. Especially for the likes of Tom. They couldn't seem to be able to take their eyes off him, or refrain from openly expressing their interest in getting to know him much more personally.

Tom was a hunk that would cause any women to jerk her head to take a second, and even a third look at him.

With a desirous gleam in her eyes, so much so I really did like the fact that he was working on second shift that was from 3:30 to midnight.

Knowing that at least I would know where he was at night, and I would have him all to myself during the day.

My problem was that I didn't know how to drive, or the driving laws in California and Tom needed the car to get to work.

So I was stuck in the apartment at night having to wait until Tom came home from work. Not knowing what he was doing. Imagining all sorts of weird things that he could be up to instead of being at work where he belonged.

I was that over protective of him when I wasn't around him to make sure some other bitch wouldn't attempt to lure him away from me.

I trusted Tom implicitly. It was the women I didn't trust to keep their gummy hands off him, or whatever else they sought to throw at him.

Tom was all man when it came to sex. Back in Milwaukee all I had to concern myself with was July through September.

Where women would be out tramping about showing off how naked they can get themselves without breaking the law. For the sole purpose of latching onto a guy like Tom to get down and dirty with him.

Where in California it was year around parading around nearly nude in revealing bathing suits showing off big tit's and nearly naked assess, and partially exposed beavers being displayed for the taking.

The beaches were flesh markets, and the streets virtual whore houses for sell. It was a Navy city where women were sold cheap by their pimps, due to the completion being so plentiful.

The women on the make were worse than cockroaches and they weren't going to get my husband from me if I had anything to say or do about it that was for damn sure.

It was going to take more than a voluptuous body to get Tom away from me. He's always been around beautiful women, and he chose me above all of them, but that wouldn't stop him from not turning down the opportunity of slipping it too them if they shoved it in his face.

* * * *

It was on a Thursdays when we first arrived. After Tom and I left his job site we stopped to have lunch. Then went apartment hunting, driving up and down the streets near where Tom was going to work. Finding a furnished studio apartment within walking distance to Tom's place of work.

We unpacked what belongings we brought with us, and went out sightseeing. We had almost three days before Tom had to be at work.

Believe me it wasn't easy for me to say no all the time, or that we can't afford it, and there was just no saying no to Tom and meaning it. Mainly because everything he took an interest in also fascinated my interest as.

When it came to a particular nighty that caught his eye especially those in Frederic's window.

I had to admit it they did look gorgeous on me as well.

Tom went ape-shit when I modeled this one two peace nighty for him. Nearly jumping me right there in the store.

"Husband are so impatient…" I spoke out to the sells women watching me holding Tom at bay. Causing me to speak out in my defense saying."

I should have known better than to bring him in here… Now you go sit back down dear, while I go change back into something not so revealing."

When I came back out. I paid for the nighty hastily and left. Practically having to drag him out of the store with him wanting to buy everything he saw, but mostly wanting touch and to see it on me.

He was like a little kid in a candy store when it came to wanting to see me in scanty risqué nighties and nylon stocking. Wanting to touch everything after I would spend time getting myself dress in it would only take him a few seconds never minutes before he was amorously attacking me.

Where he would be expecting me to endure his overbearing trifling physically tormenting me touchy feeling, and whatever dotting expecting me to just lay there, and ignore what he was doing.

Tauntingly trifling examining every inch the nighty was covering until he finally did the honorable thing to ease my torment.

On this particular night after he literally ruined a brand new outfit. He had me slip on a long coat to cover over the remains of the nighty, and dragged me out to a drive up restaurant to get us a burger and fries.

If that wasn't bad enough. After we ate he drove down to a beach and parked where he ever so passionately leaned over kissing me.

Then expecting me to sit there hoping that no one would come by and look at us. With me wearing a full length coat in the middle of August when the temperature was in the high 70's covering up what he was doing underneath it making me look eight, months pregnant.

It was nothing less than a mind boggling but, yet an overwhelming accelerating thrilling experience.

One that we never openly ever shared before out in the open, and he was driving me up a wall from utter madness. While I was trying not to show the extent of the effect he was having on me.

Tom had an insatiable impulsive side to him that at time became incredibly outrageously staggering at times that became intolerably dangerous to endure.

Tom never attempted anything so outrageous, or so daringly risky before. All because of a risqué nighty and the adverse effect it was having on him.

The utter suspense and the uncertainty of it all was sensationally spellbinding, but was it ever nerve-racking as hell.

Moving to California was having a strange effect on Tom. That was bringing about his impulsiveness. While inciting reckless inspirations.

That I was finding thrilling to a point as well as his sensationalism but, I just couldn't except that he was still the same Tom I once knew.

His recklessness and lack of concern where and when he would at empty pulling his antics was not in Tom's nature.

Back home where he knew he was in control, but here where we were both still uncertainly uncomfortable about our surrounds where he would blatantly risk exposing himself to the uncertainty of being exposed, wasn't at all like him.

There was something about him that made me feel uncomfortable with him. Like there was an absence of understanding emerging between us. That was bringing about such an erratic sudden change in him.

I admit I was finding his adventurous exploitations sensationally accelerating and it's not as if Tom and I never exhibited ourselves out in public having sex before. It was just coming on me as weird, and out of the ordinary for some reason.

Luckily nothing came about that warranted my apprehensions. It was the way it all came about all of sudden catching me totally unprepared for what he was contemplating. By not even forwarding me of his intentions.

No sooner than we got back into the apartment I asked him. Just what was his sexual antics about?

I even reprimanded him by sternly asking him what was going on with him. Trying to understand why he was acting to irresponsibly and with little if any lack of concern for me. Possibly subjecting me to possibly become totally embarrassed by his shenanigans

"What is it I asked? Has all the love gone out of our marriage that you don't find me desirable anymore. That you're resorting to becoming adventurously amorous in order to get some satisfaction out of making love to me. You could have at least said something to me before hand to prepare me for what you wanted to do."

"Honey it's a new time, and a new life for ourselves. Is it a crime to be happy, and to be somewhat reckless? It doesn't mean that I don't honor or respect you, or that I don't love you any more, or I don't find you desirable.

It's just that seeing how we're free now I'm finding myself wanting to express myself in a way that would express my sensationalism when I'm with you. If that's making any sense.

Honey, I just can't see to explain how this new freedom is making me feel! I don't know maybe it's a matter of personal pride in accomplishing what I felt was impossible...

Honey we did it...! We're out of our old life totally. We're free now... We made it...! Don't you understand that?! We can do what we want when we want to do it now...!"

"What are you raveling about...? You certainly not making any sense... You weren't the one who's honor was being offended upon. By subjecting me to making a skeptical out of myself.

If someone would have taken notice, and expect me to explain what was going on. Sitting parked right under a street light no less. Making it even more nerve-racking on me with people constantly walking about.

It was my honor that was being preyed upon by having me sit there on pins and needles like you did. By putting me on exhibit for anyone to see me making a spectacle out of myself.

You weren't the one practically naked under that coat... What if he hell were you thinking anyway?!

Subjecting me to the mental stress of having to love every villainous thrilling moment of it, especially in a place that we know nothing about. We aren't back home here.

We're here trying to make a new life for ourselves not to get arrested over something like an impulsive whim, or urge that we couth could have delighted in sharing together.

What if someone would have called the cops? What would it have accomplished besides getting us in trouble. Just so you could have your moment of getting a thrill for yourself.

Certainly not thinking of me having to patronize you.

Especially out in public in a place where we don't know nothing about that could have ruined everything for us.

I didn't come all his way with you to have to turn around and be sent back because you can't handle your impulsiveness like most moral guys do in the privacy of their own homes.

Where I can give you the thrill of your life that you'll never forget without having to worry about someone watching.

Honey, all you managed to do was get us both all worked up unable to do anything about it. Especially out in the open where everyone could see. Just asking to get us into trouble.

We are not at home anymore you are going to have to stop this stupid nonsense, and start acting like the man you're, so we can celebrate together.

Where we can both can openly express are excitement over being together at least until we both find a place where we both will be comfortable exhibiting ourselves openly.

Honey I'll make love to you anywhere I' have never deny you anything you know that, but this spontaneousness has to be concentrated where the likelihood of making a spectacle out of it is for are pleasure only.

You are really getting me worried that something bazaar is happening to you. Now after all we just went through to get here. Honey don't you dare start going crazy on me now..."

I walked towards him taking off my coat shoving him back down on the bed positioning myself sitting on top of him. Pinning him down against the mattress speaking out.

"Honey you know all one needs to do is simply ask, or suggest like you always and, and I would have been more than happy to have oblige you.

I can see now that I've spoiled you in letting you think you can take advantage of my submissiveness when it comes to appeasing your impetuousness.

Honey I never want to deny you anything the you desire from me but you could have pocked a more secluded place where I could have reciprocated. As pleasurable is it was for you all your effort did for me was to aggravating the hell out of me.

We have to be extremely careful not to break any laws or to draw attention to ourselves. I don't mean to get you upset but it's important for both of us to remain in control of our senses.

We'll find way to appease each other whims, but our happiness must come first. The last thing I want to do is place limits on you.

I want what you want just as much as you do, but I don't want anything to ever separate us ever again."

"Honey I realize now that your right and that I lost myself up in the happiness I'm experiencing. You don't understand. I never loved or felt what it was to love not even myself. I don't know of any other way to express myself emotionally.

I just became overwhelmed by my joy of finally being free to opening express myself. It wasn't my intentions to subject you to ridiculous, or to place us in harm's way.

I just don't know how to show my real feelings by putting them in words. I'm sorry I thought that you understood me but I guess I was wrong."

"No, honey I was the one that was wrong, and I've a lot to learn but I can't if you don't open yourself up to me so that I can understand what's going in inside you.

Honey what I through I did understand about you. You can't change on me now. You also have to understand I'm coming out of a very trying life that we life behind with great expectations for us to have a much better life for ourselves.

I don't want to change a thing about you. I love you just the way you're, but that new Tom just wasn't the Tom that I liked. Leave your past behind you but don't ever change being the tom who I came to love with all my heart and soul.

I just want you to know that you literally ruined my new nighty. How all that's left for me to do is to take it off and just be myself. That is unless you want to do it for me, that is...?"

CHAPTER 7

Four, more weeks past, and Tom was doing fantastic at his job and still coming home directly after work straight into my waiting arms.

Life was great, and as time moved on we felt more, and more secure in our belief that we made it, and could finally relax. Other than constantly having to worry every time a knock came to our door.

The weeks became months. Where on every Thursday, which was his payday we would go out, and have a late diner.

Our new life was working out marvelously for us. We took a chance, and it was paying off. Tom was already moving up learning the milling machines. Teaching himself every step of the way.

He bought the tools that he needed. Using his payroll deductions, and actually got his first rise. All in less than a mouths time.

We were on are way in making a new life for ourselves. We were even going to rent are first unfurnished apartment and furnish it ourselves.

We had money saved up, not much, but enough so we could go out and spend it without feeling guilty. Then it happened.

The company Tom was working for lost a large government contract, and Tom got laid off.

He couldn't draw unemployment because he didn't work a full 16 weeks to be able to collect it, nor could we get aid from welfare.

Out of fear that if we applied for it Wisconsin would discover where we were, and the company didn't even give him his $500.00 like they promised.

Saying that he didn't complete his honorary time period of one year before he would be eligible for the bonus that was promised to him upon being hired.

What appeared to be a major upset turned out to be a blessing. Tom found another job a week later.

It was for less than what he was getting, but it was with a large established company who assured him a minimum of 5 years with overtime and benefits.

Tom jumped at the job, and we were on are way again, but Tom had to work longer hours, and weekends, but there again the money was better than what he was making.

During which I even got my driver's license, and was now driving Tom back, and forth from work. Making it possible for me to have the car most of the time.

Then what I felt sure would be another major setback happened. I found myself pregnant. To my utter amazement Tom was ecstatic with the idea of becoming a father.

* * * *

It was then when I think that our life together took a major transition that bought about the turn of events that lead to the downfall of not only our marriage, but the disillusion of the love we once shared.

We were out buying baby things already, and I was only six, weeks into my pregnancy, and not really sure that I was until the doctor officially confirmed that I was for sure and I was in my sixth week.

I never saw Tom so excited about anything, or so protective of me. He dotted on my every movement.

If that wasn't bad enough. It was like pulling teeth to get him to have intercourse with me. He was that apprehensive over the babies and my welfare.

I had to keep on assuring him it was alright. Then while in my seventh mouth I miscarried while having intercourse with Tom.

Neither Tom, or I really knew that much about my body other than the obvious. The rest we relied on the doctor directions valuing his opinion.

As for my mother advising me. She never explained anything to me. Other than telling me to never let a boy insert his penis inside the opening between my leg.

Saying that place was only for my husband to insert himself into, to produce his son, or daughter. That was about the extent of my knowledge other than what I was listening from the other girls talking about amongst themselves.

As for Tom. Well, he might have gotten to know far more than me about my female parts than I did, he sure was one hell of an expert at manipulating them.

We were very sexually active as most married couples are for over three, years before I got pregnant

Before what horrifically happened that virtually terrified the hell out of both of us. Due to the shock from not knowing what happened.

When he withdrew from me. He was drenched in blood. panicky blaming himself for killing his son going literally berserk without even knowing why.

Paradoxically calling for an ambulance sending me to the hospital. Frantically crying out that he killed his child working himself into having himself a major heart attack before knowing for sure about anything.

It was at the hospital that the doctor told him that I miscarried and the baby died. Mentioning that the baby was going to be a boy.

The doctor tried to tell Tom it wasn't his fault. That the embryo logical cord got entangled around the baby's neck strangling him.

It wasn't until afterwards when Tom's love for me became twice as protective. As well as his sex drive radically increased. As if he attempting to get me pregnant again.

Three, gruelingly long tedious years later he finally seceded. During which he rose to the position of foremen, and we bought are first house.

Only to suddenly stop having intercourse after the third mouth, which then only became oral sex, and manual orgasms.

I knew why he was denying himself from having intercourse with me. To him he was refusing to let what happen to his first child happen to the one I was going to have. Sternly letting his position known why saying.

"There was no way I was going to put himself, or you for that matter. Though another miscarriage." And he meant it. No matter how hard the doctor, and I tried to convince him that it was safe to have intercourse up to the eight month.

Once a week, every week it was to the doctor I went. The doctor was seeing more of me than my own husband was.

During which Tom developed himself trend. Making a point to caress my belly lying with his head on me on my hip next to my pelvic region where he would speak loving nurturing things to the baby inside me. Driving me up a wall trifling with me but would never even attempt enter me. Not even with his little finger.

The doctor I had was a man in his late 20's. Who had the bedside manner of a practitioner, and the charm of a slob sophisticated gentlemen that came with a Swedish accent.

Along with the blond hair, and the blue eyes. Including being a powerfully structured man with a muscular build. He was obviously a man greatly admired for more that his medical credentials amongst the ladies.

Tom was working twelve, sometimes fourteen, hours a day. Making me feel as if he was trying to avoid me.

My sex life was almost down to nothing, and I was trying to be understanding and supportive, but I was only human and spoiled by very frequently tended to sexually.

Nothing would had happened if doctor Wilson wouldn't have instigated it. I was in my fifth mouth. Doctor Wilson and I would mostly sit and talk in his office while he would examine me.

Where Tom would diligently drag me to the doctor's office weekly. Where I was considering it a total a waste of time on his part. As well as an imposition on me having to get undressed and dressed unnecessary.

I admit I did become attracted to him, but it was only a harmless attraction. I never thought that it was noticeable where he was concern, until it started to become obvious that he was feeling something towards me.

By his reluctance to stand upright when he got up after examining me to stand beside me. Still lying fully exposed on the examining table from the waist down with my feet resting in stirrups.

His nurse would never remain for any length of time. On the most part she left after she prepared me to be examined, and only returned when he switched on the light. Indicating that he needed assistance.

It wasn't until this one peculiar day that Tom took me to see the doctor before my regular schedule visits because he apprehensively felt certain that something was wrong with the baby. When I was experiencing stomach cramps that I was feeling uneasy about.

Doctor Wilson and I talked extensively about Tom abstaining from having intercourse with me. He told me to get him to try.

I told him I did, and he wasn't having any part of it other than drugging and forcefully raping him.

That's when the doctor told me that the cramps were a form of a biological withdrew reaction from not having sexual intercourse.

He gave me some pills that would calm my cramps severity until my body became accustomed to being celibate.

I was always irritable, cranky and easily angered, and highly emotionally unstrung most of the times.

Making me feel at times as if a time bomb was ticking inside me on the verge of going off any second while anxiously waiting for Tom to come home so I could jump on him.

Over anything to get an argument going between us to release some of my anxieties and never-racking tensions that was building up inside of me

For over 8 years I was sexually active not going for over a few days without having intercourse with Tom even though his other forms of attentiveness were extremely satisfying. They never totally appeased me. It was as if I was addicted to being internally sexually satisfied over us having intercourse, and nothing else was doing the job.

Once Tom got involved sexually it was like going through a ritualistic orgy with him. If not satisfying my sexual needs wasn't already driving me up a wall. I couldn't help but to wonder what it was doing to him.

From the very first time Tom took my virginity. Unknown onto me when he made a woman out of me.

He resurrected the women inside of me that was lying dormant just waiting to come out. Graving every form of sexual sensation, that he bestowed upon me.

That he endearingly ingrained in me with every miraculously never-racking

DISPLACEMENT INTENT

sensation. From the mind boggling orgasmic revelation, along with the insatiable longing to be uninhibitedly unleashed.

I was a 17-year-old girl who's never been with the likes of a man like Tom. Who never really was aware about what sort of incredible man he was.

Not only because he made my firs sexual experience so wonderfully spectacular. That I never really felt any real discomfort, and only the sensationalism of the physical act itself.

I was so out of it I never gave any thought about how masculine Tom was. All that mattered to me was that I traveled in the glorious inconceivable bliss he bestowed upon me.

Each time since then reaching for the incomprehensible climax (satisfied) when we came together. Forming that inconceivable bond between each other. Finding ourselves lying in each other's arms again. That's the way it was for the past 8 years.

I had no doubt in my mind that Tom was feeling the effect from the lack of are togetherness just as much as I was, but he wasn't going to risk anything happening to his baby, or to me either for that matter.

* * * *

It happened on one of my regular visit to doctor Wilson's office. I was lying on the examining table with my feet in the stirrups.

Doctor Wilson was sitting before me on his observing stool. Feeling around every nook and cranny of my genital region, probing his fingers inside me supposedly examining me internally.

When something told me that his wasn't an examining fingers of a doctor, but of a man attempting to arouse me, and was he ever doing just that.

He was not only touching me; he was simulating spots that I knew where meant to cause tantalizing reactions. That along with feeling his warming breath upon me breathing heavily upon me.

Making me feel that he was uncomfortably too personal. That along with his pungent finger tips bluntness pressing while caressingly rubbing about the orifice he was supposed to be examining Them massaging certain highly sensitive areas. Was all I need to tell me that his stimulating finger was reflecting what he really wanted to have inside me as I felt the full extent of his finger probing around inside of me.

I was already pregnant. Tom would never know and I so desperately needed what he wanted to give me. I spoke out to him saying. "Is everything alright allowing his finger to continue examine me internally.

Causing him to raise his head up to look up into my obligingly needy eyes while increasing his fingers intensity on tantalizing me internally. Submissively excepting myself to become respondent to the sensations he was having on me.

I didn't have to say anything. He just rose up and stood before me and looked me directly into my eyes.

His intrusion didn't shock me one bit. When I felt him amorously entering me. Even though it hurt like hell. Nothing ever felt so damn good inflicting every nerve and muscle in me entire body to become so tauntingly tense.

Then instantly orgasmic to where I felt as if I was jolted by electrifying spasmodic surges being gratifyingly besieged upon throughout my entire body.

The unbearable pressure just exploded with such intensity that I thrust myself forwards and violently shuck against him from the convulsiveness of the orgasmic splendor. While I vigorously stared back at him directly into his eyes.

Responding adulterously fornicating myself, solely over the want of feeling womanly again dissolved my love for Tom.

Frivolous submitting myself to another man's desires feeling ashamed, but loving losing the resentment towards myself in the climactic bliss of becoming internally gratified again.

To me all other forms of sex could never be as accelerating fulfilling. No longer being able to tolerate Tom's abstaining from giving me what I wanted so desperately.

Doctor Wilson helped me through the most difficult time of my life. It was a time in my life when I needed Tom the most and he refused to be there for me.

Knowing why he wasn't didn't make my pregnancy any less unbearable. As hypocritical as it must sound I stilled loved Tom with all my heart. and soul.

It was a time in my life that I know what it felt like to be deserted by the one I loved. That every women who's had to suffer through for one reason, or another who knows what it feels like to go through what I was going through.

In my eyes men had no right to just make women out of us, and just up and not adhere to the obligations they alone created.

Sexually Tom wasn't there for me. Where I was expected to still be there for him. Satisfying his wants and desires, where he wasn't for me.

Just because he was afraid that I would miscarriage again wasn't an excuse enough to expect me to endure for so long.

Having to be denied especially when he was right there beside me, allowing him to persecute me for him getting me pregnant. While using it as an excuse for not loving me anymore because of it.

Doctor Wilson and I shared nothing more than a physical relationship together. He was there even though it was by appointment only. Nothing endearing, or romantic, or any attachments was formed from it.

He was in, and was out. He went his way I went mind. That was the extent of it. I knowingly knew what I was giving him, and what he was giving me in return was what I so desperately needed to make my life bearable over having to be denied.

Up until the eight month I lived a double life. Loving one man while giving myself to another, while asking myself.

'How is Tom able to refrain for so long?' Oral sex only tantalized Tom's infatuation. It never totally satisfied him sexually as much as actual intercourse did.

It was that internal inner stimulation that was Tom's sexual driving force. He had to have that internal solidarity from within to totally satisfy him.

Which made me feel certain that he was getting it from another women and that only infuriated me even more. Not knowing who, how, or if in fact he was cheating on me with some other women.

When he wasn't a work he was home with me and he always handed me his paycheck every Thursday night, and as amorously spontaneous as he always was. I wasn't letting him out of my sight.

Tom loved shooting pool that he was damn good at it. When he was restless

He loved nothing more than going too hustle at pool halls. There was no way he was going out shooting pool unless I was out there with him, and he wasn't drinking more than usual.

Tom wasn't one for stopping with the guy after work for a beer he was extremely anti-social and never let anyone get to close to him.

He trusted in no one but me, and always had me doing most of the talking when someone might drop over to chat when we were out and we would happen to meet.

It was me who was the sociable one. I needed someone when he was at work so I started becoming acquainted with the neighbor wives.

Who would on occasions bring their husbands over to meet Tom. Which really never went very well where Tom was concern.

I created a one women man, who was a home body, who's only thought was to make me happy. Who gave a rat's ass about anyone else, and didn't want to have anything to do with them? Rightfully so because Tom had nothing in common with anyone else other than those he associated with in his past life.

He didn't like sport, or mingling with other guys. He didn't like gossiping about other guys, or bragging about how many women he laid, or divulging any part of his precious life, but try to screw him over, and he would just as soon kill you rather than to tolerate you.

However, through it all Tom was becoming a law abiding citizen who did nothing illegal. That was due solely to my efforts that he was becoming an up standing human being.

I knew that he missed his previous life style a lot. He would reminisce about how it uses to be back when.

Little by little the horrors of what Tom did, and was capable of doing became known to me, and the more the truth became known the more I wish that I never heard about any of it.

What I found most disturbing was the reason behind the way Tom became so unscrupulously dangerous.

The way he did was basically because he was the bastard child of his father's brother while his father was out at sea. Tom's mother Mary had a onetime affair

DISPLACEMENT INTENT

with Tom's father brother Frank.

Mary told Norman Mary's husband that Tom was his son. Norman, Tom's father knew better and his hatred turned into contempt for Tom the second he suspected his wife cheated on him while he was off fighting during the war in the Navy

From the age of one, Tom was beaten, mentally abused, and physically tormented until he reached the age of eight, years old, and ran away from the hospital he was in.

Tom never went back home until he was force to only to run away again. He lived on the streets until he was thirteen, when he was befriended by a man who's name I can't mention.

This man adopted Tom as his own son. It was though this man that Tom got really involved in his previous life.

This man even sent him though his own training school where he started learning the martial arts at the age of thirteen.

While learning how to become a better thrift. learning the arts of safe cracking, and electronics so that he could disconnect alarms systems.

By fifteen, his benefactors were teaching him how to go about collecting from deadbeats who weren't paying their bills to him.

What was making Tom's story even worse was. By the age of 13 he already killed his first person. A cop no less. While he sat in his car eating a donut and drinking coffee.

He snuck up on him and shoved a knife up through his throat with such a force the point of it came out the top of the cop's skull, and the list of his horrid accomplishments went on from there.

Until he became a profession killer for on certain person. Amongst being this person personal bodyguard when he wasn't out working for him for the purpose of blending in with the others who were also connect with the association he was working for.

There were only three, people in Tom's life that I knew he said he could trust. That was his adopted father, Carol and I.

He never made friends mainly because he never knows when he might have to someday face them. So he always stayed to himself.

Like I said Tom didn't like people getting to close to him, and of course I could have all the friend I wanted and I quickly found out that people in California weren't anything like the peopled back in Milwaukee.

They were either snobbish, or they had ulterior motives to want to associate with you, and like the fool that I was Tom let me find out the hard way.

That California people were only out to use you and when they used me. I wouldn't dare tell Tom knowing him the way I did. He would love nothing more than to revert back to his grotesque despicable ways.

Tom was a bomb just waiting for an excuse to go off. Who looked upon people as his enemies Always knowing where he was at all the time. Just itching to call upon his guardian angel.

After three, false alarms and eighteen, hours of grueling labor are daughter Sally was born. I thought Tom would be upset that it wasn't a boy but he wasn't. He was the proudest father in all the world.

He wanted to bring Sally home the next day, but doctor Wilson wouldn't hear of it telling Tom that I had to stay at least a whole week in the hospital before he would even think of letting the two of us come home.

It wasn't until I got home that I discovered why Tom didn't put up a major fuss not demanding that I be sent home earlier.

That loving irresponsible husband of mine spent every last cent we had and took out a loan to completely decorate the entire house including the baby's nursery.

I couldn't believe Sally's bedroom. It looked like a queen's chambers where our bedroom was nothing less than a chamber of lust.

With mirrors even on the ceiling, it had red carpeting, and there sitting in the center of the room was a king size round bed with a black fur bedspread, and bright red silk pillows, and there at the foot of the bed was the must sexist negligee I ever saw lying at the foot of the bed.

Coming to find out that the panties were eatable panties. As much as I was still hurting from the stitches. There wasn't going to be no stopping me. From all that day and through the night Tom and I made love.

DISPLACEMENT INTENT

Only stopping to feed and tend to Sally then going back it again and again. Knowing that my husband was back in my loving arms again making mad passionate love to me in every conceivable way and some new ways he just thought up.

CHAPTER 8

During the three years that followed Tom continued to keep enriching our lives. I didn't have the heart to tell him that Sally was going to be his only child.

Doctor Wilson broke the bad news to me while I was in the hospital. Due to some complication involving my ovaries and he had to inform me that it would be very unlikely that I would ever be able to have any more children.

Using that as an excuse for him taking it upon himself to prevent me from getting pregnant again after Sally was born.

It wasn't until three, years later that I found out that, that devious bastard was ling to me all along and the only reason he tied off my tubs was in hopes that he would be able to continue to carry on his illicit affair with me.

Without having to concern himself about getting him getting me pregnant, and all those false pregnancies where induce by him to make me think I was pregnant and eventually miscarried again so he could continue having sex with me.

It was while I was in the hospital having my ovaries removed because of what doctor Wilson did to me that I found out from a young voluptuous woman all of twenty-five, years old about Wilson's, and his involvement with not only herm as well as numerous of other women. Along with someone else who I never expected to hear about.

My own husband Tom as well and him and how they have been collaborating together all along colluding together in some elaborate scheme that literally destroyed the happiness of the life Tom and I were sharing together along with our daughter Sally who was just now going on three, years old.

Her name was Nancy. I admit I let myself go a bit, but when I saw her and looked at myself in the mirror. I realized just how far I let myself go.

Nancy was a robotics instructor. I came to find out that Nancy worked at the same place Tom did as a secretary.

DISPLACEMENT INTENT

She was talking to several of her close friends when I heard the name Tom mentioned. She was in the hospital for an abortion that doctor Wilson himself was going to perform.

She didn't know I was Tom's wife, nor did I know it was my husband

Tom she was they were talking about at the time.

Nancy was only brought in and was expected to be leaving that afternoon after Wilson preformed the abortion that apparently wasn't her first time he performed one on her.

Tom was at work, and wasn't coming to visit me until visiting hours later that night. Nancy was lying in the bed next to mine talking to a young blond hair girl who was with several other young, and very attractive young women standing around her bedside.

I was laying behind the partially drawn curtain reading a book, but couldn't help from overhearing barely being able to see as well as hear what they were talking about

"Jesus Nancy how many times are you going to go through this for that guy?" The blond hair girl asked Nancy.

"That's none of your business Betty." Nancy argumentatively snapped back." Just because you've the hots for Tom yourself! Doesn't give you any cause to go meddling into my relationship with him!"

The second she mentioned the name Tom my heart literally stopped. Nervously asking myself.

'Could she be referring to my Tom...?! No it can't be. It just can't be... There's thousands of guys by the name of Tom...' Straining my ears to hear more.

"So what difference should it make to you Betty." Nancy snapped back in reprisals.

"He's the best thing that's ever happened to me. He's the only one that helped me get where I am now.

All you other girls were meat on the hoof to him, he's always only loved me, now of you would be where you are if it wasn't for me connecting you up with him just don't forget that. Along with the fact that I've known him long before any of you did.

You all knew that it has always been me since the day he met me. When I was assigned to work with him as his secretary, and even before I made it possible for us to all come together.

Since then it was because of me that we shared a wonderful relationship since then. Knowing that if he wasn't already married I would have been married to him now, and still having to deal solely with me.

As far as I'm concern. The way you girls flaunt yourselves in front of him. Any guy would stick it to you, like he ism and until I'm his wife I'm going to have to content myself with that, because of the position we are all in with him, and doctor Wilson.

If it wouldn't be for that none of you would mean anything to him, and I would be the only one in his life."

"Listen to me Nancy." The oriental girl interrupted Nancy speaking out." I grant you Tom is a marvelous guy, and he's helped us all out a lot of us in a great many ways, but you're not the only one being put though having an abortion.

Some of us have a lot more to loss than you do. Are husbands for one. While he's racking in magi-bucks from all of us, we're still having to foot the bill for his total disregard for us."

"That's not true!" Nancy again defiantly snapped back." And you damn well know it. He's never forced himself on any of you, or into doing anything none of you didn't want to do, and you all know it!

I know what you're all after. You're all fighting amongst yourselves to get him for yourselves. I'm not blind, or deaf, but I don't have to fight for his affections where the rest of you have too.

I was stupid. That's why I'm here. I trusted in those damn experimental birth control pill. That didn't work worth the shit, and let's not forget our family doctor Mr. Wilson having the privilege of taking liberties with all of us as well.

For all we know he could have been the one getting us all pregnant prescribing those phoney pills to us knowing that they don't work.

So stop dumping everything on Tom just because he doesn't like to wear protection!

I admit that at times it could have been all my fault when I knew it wasn't safe, but I got so lost up in what was going on I lost all sense of reality and when I regained my senses it was way past the point of no return that's now much he can affect me.

I'm not like the rest of you thinking that by getting yourselves knocked up by him would get him away from his wife, I know better.

Beside I'm not as liberal as all the rest of you are where man is concern. If you get my meaning?

I'm patient. Knowing that his wife won't be around forever meanwhile positioning myself for when she's out of his life too where I'll be the one who's going to be taking her place, and I'm warning you all right now.

If either of you, or that Janet so much as goes near his wife, or even attempts to speak to her I'll make sure you'll all regret it!

I know all about the four, of you don't forget that! He's mine, and no one, and I mean no one! is going to get him away from me.

He doesn't even know I'm here. He's coming to see me tonight at the Spa. His wife is having some operation because she's going to hell peace by peace.

Where his wife is getting flabby and falling apart I'm keeping myself young, firm and gorgeous, and a lot better for him than she could ever be, and smarter than anyone of you are.

You Betty he's helped you to get through that stupid computer school, and you Sue Wang. Where would you be now if he didn't get you that job at his place of work to get you the benefits you needed to pay for all those extensive operations you needed to keep you looking as young as you do now after your accident. So you could land that rich husband you now enjoy so much.

As for Maxi. Let's not forget miss hot to trot. Who's never got a break in her life because she was black. Who is now, thanks to his efforts. Is going to become his supervisor at work.

All of you have ulterior motives for caring about him. Where I've only one. The fact that I love him.

As much as I detest him for falling victimized to your female wiles. I can't blame him for doing so, but be warned. After this he's mine. Dare to come near him, and I'll tear your hearts out!

I got my tubs tied now so that I don't have to concern myself any longer with getting pregnant.

Nothing I tried never seemed to work with him anyway. Him and that confounded fetish of his of having to finish all the time, was trying on my nervous system. Always having to keep track when it was the safest time.

Now I don't have to give a shit any more, but I'm damn sure not going to tell him, that's for damn sure. I can ruin all of you just don't forget that.

I helped put all of you in the high positions you now hold I can just as easily get you all kicked out of them, plus have all you assess thrown in prison until you are old a gray."

"Nancy." Betty spoke up in her defense." You've us all wrong we're as fond of Tom and very appreciative of him, even though it might appear that we are in love with him, we even might be up to a point, but we aren't nearly as much as in love with him as you're.

We all know the way you feel about him, but we to have strong feelings for him. True it could be because that he has done so much for us where we weren't about to do for ourselves was as sexual you have to admit he is truly a man to be desired.

As much as we do respect and admire him as a person. If we didn't, do you think we would keep caring about him the way we do?

Especially knowing that he's involved with other women, plus the fact that he is a married man?

I'm not attempting to praise the guy but where we're finding him is nothing less than incredible on his part. For him to be able to keep up with all of us.

Look at us Nancy there's not a single one of us that's could be hard up to get any man. He means something special to all of us for a number of reasons, and damn straight sex is a major one.

But we all have to ask ourselves. Why does all of us think including you that he can get us to do what we do for him so that he can promote himself?

He could have been the supervise long before he made it possible for you to appoint Maxi into the position that he could have had and place you not only in the position above him before leaving the company he was previously at.

DISPLACEMENT INTENT

We all know that he's pimping us out to all those executives in other companies, and sitting on what we bring back for him, including you as well.

So don't go placing yourself in any high and mighty pedestal over us. Just because you think he thinks of you over all of us, because he doesn't

He's using us, and we're letting him because he is someone special too each, and everyone one of us. Whereas he's never letting us forget that we all beholding to him.

The company, along with how many maybe others like the one we're working for are practically his now as it is. We're talking five women not counting his wife.

Shouldn't that tell all of us something about the sort of guy he is and that he's not willing to settle for what he's got.

He's just letting those assholes think that they're in control of what's going on in them when he has us manipulating the figure heads by catering to them along with blackmailing them. With him excluding himself from becoming involved.

Threatening that they could destroy, not only their company. but their lives as well. While using their families as a threat against them.

It's been going on some three, years for you, and over 2 years for the rest of us. This isn't any flirtatious fling any of us have been having with him, and we all know that he's got us as well by our short hairs.

That it's been an ongoing thing that we all obviously want to continue, but the guy is caring on with six, different women, and maybe how many different women might be entering the picture we have no way of knowing. He's got himself a marketing harm and knowing him like we all do.

Along with what he has on us as well. There's no way in hell we could say no to him. Even if we wanted too. Just to put all of our positions into perspective to where we might also stand where he's concern.

He's human, there's no way he can go on continuing at the rate he's going to much longer. Where we can't risk him wanting to stop coming to us for more.

I for one wants him to back off, and so does Maxi here. That's why we came to talk to you. We've all been discussing him and none of us can risk hurting his feeling, and none of us can say no, to him sexually or otherwise.

The hell with owning him. It the sex he's using on me to get me to do what I do for him, and I feel that I have more than paid him with interest for what he's done for me.

I'm going to be marrying Ted in a month so what in the hell am I going to do after I do marry him?

Ted's by no mean any dummy. He'll know if I'm screwing around on him. He'll find out just like we do, by taste, examining, and my sexual response, or my lack of enthusiasm after I come home from a long trying time at work. He's not the greatest lover in the world I'll have you all know, but he's a damn nice, rich guy that I really care for.

I'm telling you having Tom around is no damn good for any of us. We've to do something to protect ourselves to let Nancy here have him, seeing how she want him for yourself so badly."

"Betty." Nancy interrupted her speaking up." Just tell Tom how you feel he'll understand."

"How could he Nancy? When I don't even understand how I could be letting a man like Tom get away, and settling for a guy like Ted, but I can't depend on my present future lasting for very much longer. So I'm going to settle while I still can.

I honestly hate letting you have Tom, but I just can't be a friend to Tom so spear me your threats they don't intimidate me one bit.

However, that still doesn't resolve the issue that like it, or not nothing going to change the way it is right now for any of us.

As much as you want to claim sole ownership Nancy it's never going to happen. It hasn't happening with his present wife, and it's not going to happen with you. So you best set you mind to that fact.

What we all need to be concerning ourselves about is how we can manipulate him to become less interested in us, and concentrate on getting what it is he has on all of us. Before something happens to screw things up from the way things are right now.

We've are own lives to consider here We've to really ask ourselves. Is he really worth allowing him to dominate the lives of five, women in the prime of their lives?

As for me as for the life of me I still can't figure out how he managed to manipulate me into the position that he's got me right now?"

"You do have a good point their Betty one I've to admit I as well have been doing a lot of thinking about." Maxi interjected giving her opinion.

"You know honestly if I didn't feel all that obligated to him for all he's done for me I really wouldn't be putting up with his bull-shit.

Sure I would do him maybe once or twice, but look at me… He's got me doing him knowingly knowing that he's also doing all of you as well.

If that isn't bad enough he's having me doctoring his time cards, and even covering for him when he doesn't even work for the company anymore, and even paying for the motel rooms he's been dragging us all off too, using the company's money.

Doing the same things, he had Nancy doing before she left after him becoming his private secretary at the firm where he's supposed to be work at right now.

I don't know how he managing all of us too get us to do the things he wants us to do. Not to mention where I just can't say no to him.

Then let's not forget about Janet, and how he's sneaking her into are family circle. Telling us that it's only business where she's concern.

I for one also had just about had enough, but I've became so involved with him and accepted so much already.

Not to mention all I've done for him that's illegal too where I feel that he's got me by my short hairs worse than he has the rest of all of you. He's got so much against me."

"Come on ladies let's not go there." Nancy spoke up jumping in on what Maxi just said." I've more to loss than all of you where that's concerned."

"Alright everyone." Betty spoke up again." I hear you, but we only have ourselves to blame for putting ourselves where we all are, and I for one have no intentions of spending any time wasting my life away sitting behind bars in some prison cell.

As far as I'm concerned I don't want to hear any more about it, and it's not going to do any of us any good to start worrying about it now. Especially conspiring to plot against him.

He's hasn't said, or suggested anything of that nature against any of us, and let's not forget. We have just as much on me as he has on us, and besides Tom's not the sort of guy that going to do something so stupid. The guy would be crazy to risk throwing away the best thing he has going for him in his life.

Not when he's got it made with us doing for him whatever he wants us to do, and we'll have to admit he is making us all very rich in the process.

So let's stop complaining and just keep on with things as they're. As I see it there's not one who is getting hurt by us association with each other.

Even through he's getting more out of this arrangement than we're, or so it might appear that he is. The way I'm seeing are position is that we're trying to compete with a man using both his brains against us and knows how to sue them to benefit him as well as us.

So until something radically changes none of us including him are in the position to attempt to change anything.

I'm certain that you all are doing our own thing outside the pack to insure our welfare in the event anything might happen between now, and whenever something might come up.

I know I consider us all one big happy family. Seeing how I know all of you as intimately as you all know me.

So there should be no reason for any jealousy or feeling threatened by either one of us. I know I'm not harboring any ill-will or doubts concerning any of you.

"We all hear you Betty, but that doesn't change are situation any." Maxi spoke up attempting to address her concerns where Tom was concern.

" In case you haven't notice I'm a different color than you, and Nancy are. With Tom in my life and with my husband being a colored as I am.

Just suppose he should get or hasn't already gotten me pregnant. That thanks to doc Wilson taking care of hasn't already happened

How will I know who's baby it's going to be if something should happen to doc, Wilson taking care of things.

If I don't do something about it to make sure I don't get pregnant, and the baby should come out white?

I'm not only going to loss myself a husband, but also be the mother of a white baby as well. I'm risking a hell of a lot continuing my affair with Tom. Let's not forget about that shall we."

Betty spoke up speaking her mind." Maxi as much as I can sympathize with you where that's concern. All I can say is you're stuck in the same situation that going to be constantly changing.

You forget not all the man we are getting ourselves involved with aren't all white. So we all run the same risks, which we all created knowingly for ourselves.

You're not the only one facing that same dilemma I'm married too, and I could still wind up facing the same situation as you.

If my husband decided to have a blood test if he having any doubts that the baby wasn't his.

As much as I respect and admire Tom and the rest of you it's getting to the point where it's jeopardizing my marriage as well.

With Tom having to call upon me unexpectedly knowing what's going to be expected of me to do too get what he wants.

Believe me you're not alone when it comes to thinking on that line. Where I myself am force to ask myself. 'Where was that concern when we all first started to get ourselves involved with Tom?'

It's not as if he forced us into having sex with him. As I recall I was sort of encouraging him too doing so. By the way I hear all of you telling me. So were all of you as well.

My husband is beginning to want to have kids, and even through the pill didn't work for you Nancy I can't go off it. I sure as hell don't want to have any kids, and it's not as if I haven't found myself in the same situation as Nancy is right now...

Having babies distorts the hell out of a women body. It's bad enough that I've to tolerate what goes in me at times. I damn sure want to be able to control what comes out of me... Maybe when I'm 90... Maybe I said..."

The way I'm looking at this arrangement is that I've a damn good things going for me here. I don't mine in the least sharing Tom with either of you.

It's my husband that I'm having trouble with hiding everything from him.

Especially the money I've been accumulating over the past couple of years.

Tom and this body of mine has gotten me very well set in my life, and I want to get even better set for my old age.

A girl can never have enough money, or sexual attention the way I see it, and I've became accustomed to living a very comfortable life style. Without having to depend on the moderate income my husband makes.

All of you too can dicker back and forth between each other, as for me I'm not going to ever say no, too Tom.

As for my husband. I'm sorry, as much as I want to I can't stop wanting to be with Tom especially now with the security I have and the ability to continue to applying towards it there's no way I'm going to be doing that. I like where I'm working, and with who I'm working with.

As far as Tom is concern I know I'm the one who's in the position of keeping our relationship going. He never placed any demands on me that I resented him for during or afterwards. and it's only physical between us.

When it does become physical between Tom and me he treats me with respect, integrity, and dignity and he not only honors me as a person but anoints me sexually.

I know that I can talk to Tom and he'll listen to me where my husband doesn't listen unless he can have things his way.

Where my husband takes me for granted, and just uses me to appease himself. There's no comparison between the two of them. Tom is my first and foremost priority.

I guess that about covers it, and the more I hear all of you talking the more I find myself regretting going along with this resentment towards him.

What about you Sue Wang. You just been standing there saying nothing. You've just as much a voice in all this as we all do.

"Well, if you must know the truth as you all know I do have a husband who loves, honors, and respects me.

Where our indifference lies, is that I'm American born, and he's mind set is an old back home one and he's set in his ways and traditions.

DISPLACEMENT INTENT

I'm the first to admit. I am a selfish minded person. I like my freedom and not having to account for where I go, and what I do.

I like going about my own house practically naked. Not having to wear those damn sarongs, or catering to my husband having to bowl, and kneel before him all the time, but I married the man knowing his ways and traditions.

I also love the freedom of spending my own money. Not bringing it home to give to him where I worked my ass for it, Where I can say in all honestly I do, and well worth every cent I get for doing it.

Tom has given me the freedom to be my own person along with all the money I want to spend.

He's also a very rewarding person, and he sincerely does cares about me. In as much as he lets me do whatever I please, when I please. Whether he likes or dislikes the decision I make

He's also always been compassionate unselfish person when it comes to love making.

There's nothing traditional about him when it comes to that.

It's more ritualistic if anything else, but I'm honored bond to my husband even as much as I do want to leave him I can't.

After my accident my husband saw me as ugly and grotesque. Where Tom went beneath the surface, and brought out the beauty in me again. Without him I could have never of went through all those operations too look the way I do now. I know that none of you ever knew this. But before my accident Tom and I were only close acquaintance there was never anything going on between us.

He came to visit me in the hospital he really felt sorry for me and truly wanted to help me recover from the massive burns I suffer in the fire of the burning car.

He uses his influence to get the doctors to treat me regardless of the cost they incurred doing it.

Taking over a year before I discovered how the miracle was able to come about.

Where my own husband rarely even came to visit me tom was there for me encouraging me not to give up.

I'm owing to that man for everything he's done for me and if it wasn't for Tom I would have left my husband long ago.

I talked to him about leaving him and he said that it was my decision to make. That before I did anything he wanted to insure I would be happy either way.

The burns I suffered covered my chest and even my pelvic region. It took major skin grafting to repair the damage tissue.

The augmentations had to cost a fortune but what was terrifying me the most was if I could ever be admired as a woman again not only visually but physically as well.

Tom constantly kept telling me how beauty I was. I blatantly told him that I didn't believe me saying. "That if you think I'm so beautiful. Prove it to me. Make love to me…"

He never hesitated for a second. When doing so he made me become alive again. So much so I never wanted him to stop making love to me.

There's a lot more that none of you don't know went on between us that makes my being here amongst the rest of you distasteful to a degree but a knowing one knowing that we all share something in common with Tom that sex alone isn't the reason why we are here.

It for that very reason I don't harbor distaste and contempt towards any of you, and nothing but my gratitude towards Tom as you all should for doing what he alone has done for all of you and myself knowing I could walk away at any time I chose to.

Where you say you've more than paid him for what you have been doing for him. Where I could never place a value on anything I would do for him.

Although I am confused as to what ends he's trying to achieve. I harbor no doubts about my love and sincerity for him. That's why I remained salient.

Other than to say. There's nothing anyone could say, or do that would keep me from going to him.

Let's face it, all of us have are reasons for wanting him, and none of us wants to give him up, nor will we.

Nancy we all know how it was that you and Tom came together, and how it was that Tom was able to help you buy that Health Spa.

DISPLACEMENT INTENT

He showed you the way how to get three, times your pay where you've been embezzling from the company ever since even while working in another company as his secretary.

Let's all stop lying to each other. We all know how this all came about from the very beginning, and while he was forming are family enterprise with us his private conspirators.

Where all of us knowingly approached him because you were sexually attracted to him knowing that he was a married man, and sought to take advantage of the time we found him most venerable to do so.

What we all never counted on was that he was far more than anyone of us expected him to be and allowed him to use us because we thought that he was capable of rewardingly fulfilling even are ambitions for us to become rich and influential.

Tom's no martyr so let's not make him out to be one. He was just a little bit harder to find out what he was all about underneath that closed up exterior wall he was protecting himself behind.

We all saw the same thing in Tom as a man what we never knew that he was also a damn genius. And was a guy that knew what, and how to achieve something incredible that's place us all in the position we are right now.

Where what attracted us to him was strictly out of our own curiosity that attracted us to him to begin with.

None of us were getting nowhere in are jobs, but getting royally screwed by our and his bosses, and when we all discovered that Tom had potential to get us somewhere we jumped at the opportunity with are skirts held up above our waists, and it paid off.

What I see now is greed. and unwise deception thinking that you don't need him anymore. So go ahead and tell him that you want out.

What are you willing to bet that he wouldn't saying to discourage any of you? He never places any demand or holds on any one of us before.

As for as his involvement as women. I honestly believed that it will be us who will wind up regretting going our separate ways.

Do anyone of you think that Tom would have any trouble getting women to replace us? I don't, so go for it. I'll stay right where I am.

Especially you Nancy when it was Tom who made it possible to get the chance to buy the places you now own.

When you didn't have the money, and you went to Tom begging him to use his influence to connect you with someone who would get you the loan you needed to buy those places.

Where now the way you are going to express your appreciation is by actually going to be placing demands upon me. By threatening all of us to deny him but yet expecting him to continue collaborating with us. Is that it?

Thinking that we would honestly be naive enough to believe you when you say you want him for yourself. Hell girl we all want that. What fools do you take us for?! He's as much as are golden eye goose as he is yours...

I know how it was between you and Tom at first. How you thought yourself to be so beautiful that no man would turn you down, but he did.

That to this day. I still don't know how it was you found out about his personal situation with his wife, but you did, and you used it to win him over my praying on his affliction that came as no secret to anyone of us.

You found out about how fearful he was to have intercourse with his wife because he blamed himself for killing his only son, by causing her miscarriage while having intercourse with her.

When his wife got herself pregnant again, and he confided in you that he wasn't going to do it again when she was with child, and you took full advantage of him by opening yourself up sexually to him when you knew he was venerable. Even though he was still in love with his wife.

All the time not knowing that you were using his aggravation just so you could listen to him while you were appeasing his denial to his wife, and you just loved how he would open up to you.

You manipulated him out of his pant into yours and all it took was just that one time for you to patronize his manly needs to hook him in.

To get him to tell you how to go about making up extra time cards. Seeing now you were the one distributing the paychecks to the departments for you and him both.

DISPLACEMENT INTENT

By using the names of people who've already been fired. To pay yourself plus even paying yourself their overtime.

Netting yourself a good $900.00 to $1,500.00 per week while he would cover for you by pouching their time cards daily and you him and letting him having to account for their lack of productivity.

The two of you had yourself something great going for yourselves where he never asks you for a dime as long as you keep opening yourself up to him.

He even took pictures of you screwing the top brass of the company to help you set him up for you so you could use those pictures to blackmail them. While he never asks you for any of the money for you to even get more money out of them.

Where it all started to go bad for you. Was when you fail in love with him, but he didn't with you, and that infuriated you. That's when you weren't willing to settle for what you got out of him.

You wanted him then for yourself as badly as you do now. Over the fact that you can't stand him not loving you like he does his wife, and you've been working to that end ever since to break the two, of them up.

Just like all the rest of us have been doing against you when we started getting involved with him.

Especially when more and more of us came into the picture. Where it became an even more compelling obsession with you to be the only one.

You've always been envious of us, because you didn't want the competition. You also became resentfully jealous of each and every one of us, and conspired to corrupt our feeling towards him by creating distention between us.

By praying on are innermost concerns regarding him and our personal lives. Out of wanting him to recognize you over us

You ever thought to go to Tom's wife and tell her all about us, but you couldn't because he knew about you embezzling hundreds of thousands of dollars over the years from the company you have been working for.

Then only to discover that there was nothing you could do to disrupt what we all had going for ourselves with him without yourself winding up in prison as well.

I don't believe that you ever really loved Tom, but regardless I'm telling you here and now/ Forget it! We're here to stay and anymore attempts to disrupt what we all have going for us you'll find yourself having to deal with me, and I'm all bitch!

I personally know Tom is no martyr, and you don't want to know what it is I know to be able to say that, but I'll say this much. How I found out was because he was looking out for all of us. You might think you know him, but you know nothing about him, and if any of you think that he's the one using us you best think again.

True he is in it for himself just as we are, but without him being in the position where he is. None of us would be here together right now, but most likely behind prison bars."

"Alright so we all know where we stand." Nancy defensively spoke up trying to get the attention off her." What about Janet. Just were does she stand in all this…?"

"As for Janet." Betty spoke up speaking for herself." As much as I detest having to put up with her, as well as all the rest of you, and all this bickering, and conspiring going on between us, and I don't like it in the least her being brought into our private organization of ours.

She's apparently with us now, and only time will tell what she's gotten Tom to do for her, or the other way around.

If it wasn't for him being such a sap. I don't think anyone of us would be here right now ourselves, but that's just the type of guy Tom is.

I'm the last person who want to stop Tom from being the kind of guy he is. I only want to slow him down some.

He's far from being any saint that's for sure, but he's done alright by me, where I can't speak for the rest of you, but he obviously has, or had something going on with all of you, and her as well.

My most prevalent concern is that something bad is bound to happen with more people becoming involved with all of us.

That's why I don't like not being as tightly met as we were when we all first came involved with each other, and we're separating wider, and wider apart from each other because of all the deception going on between us.

We're all living alternate life styles with some of us being married, while others are obviously carrying on other relationships outside those we're already carrying on.

This whole thing that is going on. Is bond to blowup in all are faces if things continue to go on the way they are. If we had any sense, we would get out now while the getting is good.

With us all being at each other's throats. It's not going to take much to totally disrupt the apple cart, and ruin everything for all of us.

I can assure you right now it does concern me a lot where it should all the rest of you. I'm thinking that what we're doing is getting to big for us to handle, and I'm for telling Tom that we need to slow down before something goes wrong.

All of us can loss everything we worked for too achieve here, and we need to all put are heads together and figure out a way to stop anyone else from getting at Tom. Making us even more venerable than we already are.

I say that we bring it up to him. Let's admit it, we're all getting greedier, and we don't have what we have going for us under are control. Even knowing what he'll probably come out and say is.

"Come on relax. I've it under control. There's nothing to worry about." Tom's no different than us. He's as greedy as hell, and most likely tell us that nothing happened yet, and won't if we just keep handling things the way we are. Where we all have more than him cheating on his wife to concern ourselves about.

Eventually someone is going to discover what's been going on and if and when that happens all it's going to take if they get to one of us. They will get to all of us. None of us aren't about to go down without coping a plea bargain and we all know it.

Then there's the "What If "Where we all know how Tom feels about the one child he already lost. What If, he finds out that we have been out killing off any of his other kids? There's no telling what he might do then.

We all know it just hasn't been only business, and nothing more where we are concern and if even catches on to what Wilson is doing behind his back. He going to pressure him to tell everything about us."

"Betty is right about that." Maxi spoke up in defending what she just said." Tom is irresponsible and unpredictable as hell. Betty is right on that score."

"Well the way I see it." Sue Wang spoke up speaking out her opinion." Nothing happened yet, and until it does I don't see any need to concern ourselves. Beside how is he going to find out it could have been his when he's got us doing what we're doing with others besides him?

We've been handling things so far without even are own husband learning about any of it and no one is going to be telling him anything that goes on between just us.

As for Nancy here. Nancy if I were you I would let sleeping dogs lie, and forget about getting over on Tom's wife.

The way I see it. If you haven't got him by now with the way you look and cater to him, it's never going to happen. Just don't bring any of us into any of it. We'll handle our own affairs where Tom is concern. Just keep that in mind if you even think of double crossing me.

The way I see it. If you can't handle the pressure disappear, and write sometime, and have done with it. I don't see him going out of his way looking for you. Just leave me out of it when you do."

"Sorry Nancy." One after the other spoke up agreeing with what Swung just said.

" Maxi was on the verge of speaking up to say something. Only to be abruptly interrupted by an orderly entering the room. Pushing a gurney up to Nancy's bedside saying.

"It's your turn lady... Seems to be the thing of the day today. Sorry ladies she has to go now..."

He stood looking Maxi, and Betty over really good saying. As Nancy climbed upon the gurney while Sue Wang stood beside the others at the foot Nancy's bed. Waiting for the orderly to wheel Nancy out of the room.

* * * *

I laid in bed fighting with myself not to believe what I was thinking, but losing the struggle as I watched them leaving. Leaving me without any doubt in my mind that it was Tom they were talking about.

Feeling cheated, and betrayed. All I could think about is how to make him pay for cheating on me I hated him that much.

That's when I came upon how I was going to pay him back. I was going to kill him with attentiveness. Using the means that would slowly kill him. Because I wanted to watch him suffer excruciatingly inch by inch day by day.

I sadistically wanted to see him die slowly before my eyes... Wanting him to pay dearly for cheating on me... angrily speaking out to myself.

'That bastard wasn't satisfied with cheating on me with just one other women. He had to do it with 5 others... That ever so damn noble contemptible sex crave hypocrite...Was going to pay dearly for his infidelity and it would be all legal. I was going to poison him...'

CHAPTER 9

I laid in bed talking to Nancy as she gets dressed to leave the hospital. Nancy looked better than I did when I first met Tom. I wanted to claw her eyes out and tear her to shreds...!

"Nancy I couldn't help but overhear your conversation you were having with your friends. Not all of it but some of it, and I must say that man you were talking about is hard to be believed."

"You can say that again he's no ordinary guy I'll say that for him. I wouldn't have put myself though getting an abortion at my own expense for just any ordinary guy.

Damn! I hope I don't show..."

She reached down hand pressing her pelvic region looking over at me asking." Does it look puffy to you...?" Turning sideways holding her hands on her hips projecting out her pelvic region.

"Somewhat, but he'll never notice..."

"He'll notice alright... Damn..., those quicken quake doctors...! I should have known better to think to be more careful. After all I've being doing for him all this time. Now he really screwed up my evening."

"Don't you think it's a bit soon to be thinking of having sex with him...?" I inquisitively ask her.

"Hell no, in fact there's no better time. There's no way he could get me pregnant again now that's for sure. Believe me having my tubes tied really puts my mind at ease knowing I can't get pregnant until I want too.

If you have any sense at all you would do the same thing. Believe it's going to make it far more enjoyable not to mention pleasurable especially where my Tom is concern. That guy is as fertile and as he is abundantly virile.

Of course I'm still going to have to fake having my period, but that only last five days, and I'm used to having to wait. He's not one for having intercourse then.

Never the less I still have my boss to contend with. For all the good he does me leaving me frustrated as hell all the time.

"Nancy do you think you could use another student at your health spa. I'm getting sort of out of shape."

"Sure I'll give you my card come in anytime." She slipped into white panties saying.

"I'll have you looking as good as new in no time."

"I'll do that. Tell me Nancy you're so beautiful. What are you doing getting involved with a married man where you could have you pick of any guy out there?"

"I have that any guy, and all guys put together in one package the day I met Tom. Tom was the day I give up the any guy, and got myself the best of all guys."

"The way I heard it you don't exactly have him."

"Oh, I got him alright. Not even his wife does for him like I do for him. As for those other bitches.

They're just holes to him. That he uses to get me jealous something, so he can get what he really wants from me. There's no way they could ever give him what I give me.

He's no fool he knows where his true desire lies. As marvelous as he is, he's still all man and I know where to keep him just where I want him, and now without having to worry about for how long, or how many times as long as I get what I want out of him. Men like him don't come by easily and I'm going to make sure he keeps coming to me.

No other women come better than me. I got the looks, the body, and the brains. What more could he ever want for in a woman than me." She vainly replied." Not forgetting to mention. "No offence intended you understand. "

But when it comes to pussies I have the best pussy of them all. I keep it tight just so he can smuggle up inside and linger for as long as he wants to where I can make it contract, and expand fluttering to keep him appeased. Where those others are loose and sloppy, and most likely all dried up

It's all in muscle control. Muscle dexterity gives him double the pleasure..." She slipped on her skirt vainly saying.

"I must be leaving now..." She picked up her purse to pull out one of her card. Walking up to me handing it to me." I hope to see you soon I'll be looking for you." She arrogantly spoke out walking towards the door then out it.

I laid in bed plotting my every move, breaking them down into stages. Feeling hollow inside as if I had no feelings, and no life left inside me.

I didn't want to stop loving Tom I just couldn't anymore... The longer I laid in that damn bed staring over at Nancy's bed, and the fact that one of the very women Tom was cheating on me with was lying right beside me, the more ferrous I became.

Suddenly finding myself finding myself not trying to find fault in what Tom did, but in what he was still continuing to do.

Where his fault lied was that he continued to carry on his affairs while telling me that he loved me. Knowing all the time he was cheating on me substituting another women body. While denying me what was rightfully mind to have.

While blatantly still expecting me to satisfy him in other ways. When unknowingly he was having assorted sex previously with another woman.

The very thought of it made me want to vomit as irately asking myself. 'How could he do such a disguising, deplorable thing to me?!'

As badly as I felt I still didn't want to resign myself to losing him to any other women. I invested over 11 years of my life with that man, and no one was going to get him away from me. Not until I was finished with him!

I wanted what was rightfully mine his worldly assets. He owed me, and his daughter that much. Then they could have what was left of him after I got through with him.

I could understand how he could have become involved. That jerk was only trying to help them out as well as himself.

He needed a way to be able to come and go freely and he used Nancy to do it by faking his time cards and filling in for him when he was out doing only what he alone wanted to do behind my back. So that I would never catch him in the act of doing whatever he was up too.

DISPLACEMENT INTENT

I felt all along that he had to be cheating on me. All those women where gorgeous, and ambitious and as venerable as he was.

He was using them so he could create his own private enterprise that I had to admit was financially paid off. Not only economically, but netted him the prestige and myself the recognition he wanted us to have.

Tom was only human, saying no isn't in his nature, nor would it be for any other guy, and California was full of exceptionally beautiful women. All wanting to grab hold of that golden ring to secure their future.

Knowing Tom, the way I did I knew that where he was concern. Once they grabbed hold of him, he was going to cash in on their true value to enrich himself.

I was starting to think of excuses that might justify his actions. Placing the blame on the women, and not on him. Actually hoping to find forgiveness for him, but the word of his philandering cut so deep into my heart that they virtually ripped out my very soul.

I also knew it was hypocritical on my part. Looking back at what I was doing with the doctor Wilson. With Tom right out in the waiting room, but him continuing afterwards is what was galling me.

Once again trying to excuse myself for continuing to appease Wilson for continuing to make sure before and after my daughter was born. Too see to it that I wasn't able to get pregnant again by tying off my tubes, and keeping his mouth shut about what was going on between the two of us.

Tom was making damn good money over 70 grands a year and in the 1970's that was allowing us to live an extravagant life style, and that wasn't counting the money he was stashing away.

Knowing him, and from what I was hearing that the amount could run up into the hundreds of thousands of dollars as well.

I wasn't about to hand that over to anyone else. Along with the benefits that came with him, including his life insurance policy.

Mentally calculating his worth could run into the hundreds of thousands of dollars more than I already knew about.

I figured that my plan of getting back at him would take a minimum of 5 years to kill him without being charged for his murder. Think that during that time who knows what might happen to him.

In the meantime, I'll be living in comfort contemplating that just maybe his life insurance would be tripled.

That I could always upgrade his life insurance policy without him knowing about it. He never looks at anything I ask him to sign.

The key to my plan was simple. I was going to slowly overdose him on chemical food additives. Mixed with bacteria, that would cause blood clogs and appear as if he had himself a heart attack.

That would attack his arteries slowly building up in his arteries as the probable cause for inducing a heart attack, or stroke.

Attacks that would eventually kill him leaving no tease of intent, and I would have no problem collecting on his life insurance policies.

Knowing that he always trusted what I cooked, or I had cooked for him, and left in the refrigerator.

Those along with adding a lot of salt, starches and cholesterol additives, and added extras like bad snack food. Like fish and pottery that would slowly achieve my goal without detection of foul play

Anything that would cause him to have a heart attack from an induced blood clogs, or maybe even a stroke that would immobilize him. Then all I had to do was wait until he was dead, and call an ambulance.

Tom already had two unhealthy vises smoking, and his drinking. As for exercise he gets that practically every day with me.

Hell I only needed a man for one thing. I could live without the love of one, or the responsibility of having to cater to one. Then there was still the artificial devise I could fall back onto if I needed to.

I would still be young enough of find someone else while still living in comfort. Maybe I'll even start myself a business of some kind.

Physically Tom was as strong as a bull. A bit sagely in spots, but that's what he was going to the Spa for too rectify, so he says. To think I would drive him and pick him up... That bastard sure had his quicken nerve...!"

DISPLACEMENT INTENT

I looked at the address on the card Nancy gave me. It wasn't the same address that I took Tom to, but the name was the same. That meant that she owned more than one health Spa.

I wanted to get all those sluts' for ruining my life, and I was willing to settle for them to suffer like I was now suffering, but I wanted then to suffer even more so.

Figuring the sicker he got. The hard it would be for them to get too him, and eventually they too would lose interest in having sex with him just like I will vet suffering through myself but not as much being the one who will be getting to him first before they even get close to him.

What really gulled me the most was. I didn't know what all Tom was sharing with them. Before he would come home and make love to me.

The thought of him being sexually involved with them continuously kept coming into my mind. Causing my throat to gag while making my skin crawl. Thinking how grotesques it could had been for me. If he didn't practice good hygiene afterwards.

* * * *

I went into surgery and was back in my room before visiting hours. Tom hired a temporary live in baby sitter to care for Sally.

I was still under heavy sedation, but I knew Tom was sitting beside me holding my hand. I laid their blaming doctor Wilson for me no longer being a total woman actually being grateful. That I wasn't able to have children from Tom, and not having to lie to Tom anymore about not being able to have any more kids.

Wilson's self-serving method was easily repaired, but not without a cost to me internally, and there wasn't a damn thing I could do about it under the circumstances.

If I did something and the truth became out with me knowing about what the two of us were knowingly doing inside that examining room behind Tom's back.

My marriage would be definitely over with Tom, and Tom would most likely wind up behind bar for killing Wilson for what he did to me. Literally denying him from having any more children from me.

The scars of what Tom's abstaining did to me will torment me for the rest of my life. I was nothing inside but the emptiness I would have to continue to shear with Tom sexually.

Losing my identity as a women leaving me feel so spiteful in all my life knowingly having to be persecuted for being admired as myself being a total woman. Wanting nothing more than to find a way to get my revenge on Dr. Wilson without being discovered for my infidelity to Tom.

I looked over into his blue eyes with nothing but loathing for him. In my mind Tom was the most despicable excuse for a human being that ever lived on the face of the earth.

My love for him was gone and now all he had was my body and determination to reap my revenge for him betraying me. As hypocritical as it even sounds to me I found myself blaming him for what I did to myself.

Looking at him pretending that he cared about me. Made me want to kill him right there and then, but there was no way I was going to deprive myself of the sadistic satisfaction of watching him slowly die before my eyes.

All I could see to thing about was watching him deteriorating slowly, struggling. As I anxiously watched him not knowing what was befalling him.

That thought and that thought alone was going to be my ultimate satisfaction. Just knowing that he was deserving of my contempt, and that I was the one that he betrayed who did it to him.

"Hi, honey..." I drowsily spoke out getting his eyes attention."

"Hi, there honey..." He replied sympathetically." The doctor said you're doing just fine and that the operation went without any complication."

He consolingly rose up leaning over kissing me then went to sit back down in the chair beside my bed.

"Maybe for the doctor it did, but I sure don't feel very womanly..."

"Honey it had to be done... Now we went through this before. It doesn't change anything I love you still as much as I always have, and you're still the most gorgeous, and the most desirable person in my life.

Being unable to have any more children really doesn't matter to me as much as I'll still have you and Sally, and you're still with me.

You've already blessed me with Sally. Which is far more than any other women could have done. You've reincarnated yourself in her and filled my heart with overwhelming joy...

I rather have you than any amount of children I love you so very much... Honey I wouldn't know what to do without you... You're my whole life...

Being able to have children wasn't what made you as marvelous as you're, and soon you'll be your old wonderful gorgeous self again, and we'll go back to living our life just the way we always have.

I still think that he talked you into doing this to yourself, and I'm having trouble not making him pay for what he did to you."

"No, Tom you can't do anything. It won't change anything. I'm alright now that's all that matters. How is Sally doing? I miss her."

"She's doing great and she misses you. I wanted to being her with me but they won't let her come to see you."

"It's better that she doesn't see me like this... Tom I don't want anyone to know about this."

"I understand honey. You know me I never say anything to anyone."

"Yes, I know. Least of all to me at times..."

"Honey I tell you everything. You know everything there is about what I do I've never given you any reason to doubt me, or my love for you."

"It's not your love I'm worrying about I know I've that. It's me. I'm not getting any younger and I'm falling apart...

Tom I know that I'm not so young and attractive looking as I was when we met, and I don't want to lose you..."

"Honey that will never happen as for being young I've done a lot of growing up these past years right along with you.

I don't want a young girl. I want the women who I married, and grow over the years with. As for being unattractive no women could equal your splendor.

Believe me honey no man or God himself could be as blessed as you have me." He rose to lean over kissing me passionately this time...

His words poured into my heart, but then became attacked by what was in my mind. Knowing that his love for me was being shared by others where I had to have all his love, or not at all, and even then.

I still wasn't sure that it would enough to get me to believe that his love for me was really real as it was when we first fell in love.

Our life these past 11 years wasn't all that easy. We had been heated moments as well as are precious ones, but nothing was as un-rectifiable as his cheating on me.

As much as I wanted to forgive, and forget all about what I heard I couldn't, and there I was pretending to be his loving affectionate wife. Kissing him back passionately hugging him up tightly against me.

Fattening my chest against his, feeling his cheating heart every despicable beat pounding against me, as my heart was being shattered inside beneath his.

* * * *

I returned home a week later, being greeted by the live in baby sitter Alice who agreed to stay on another couple weeks while I recuperated.

Having to impatiently wait until after she left before implementing my diabolical plot to do away with Tom. By first attacking his beer consumption habit.

By buying him twelve, packs instead of 6 packs making sure I put his beer in a glass in which I first started to add small amounts of salt.

Increasing it gradually adding a small amount of bio-bacteria using the salt to cover up the taste. Such a polluted water that I took oft of the garden where I sprayed insecticide to kill the bugs and insects

Then proceeded onto phase two. By personally preparing him greasy foods like bacon, and buying cheap Hamburg, and always giving him lots, and lots of margarine instead of butter.

I piled it on everything. Adding it even to the bad food that left out intentionally such as exposed hamburger, and bits of pottery. That I let sit out for hours even a day at time.

Not enough to kill him prematurely just enough to make the poison grow slowly to infect his nervous system, arteries, and muscularity.

I cooked him fresh bread soaked in butter. Lots of butter... Ham, eggs, no less than 4 eggs, and more bacon, lots of bacon... That was drenched in grease. He loved his bacon.

While even feeding myself the same things, but making it a point to drink tons of water to keep flushing my system out, and by eating lot less portions.

Watching him become sluggishly weaker, and increasingly disenchanted sexually as the mouths went by. Before adding small amounts of toxic chemicals, and maybe a drop but not anymore to only the foods that I knew he would love to snack on. Nothing that anyone else would enjoy eating.

Kicking it up a notch or two by accidentally leaving out tuna, ham, and chicken out for him to snack on when he got home.

Knowing that he was building up an intolerance towards eating bad fool, but not against the bacteria that I was purposely adding to his food before bringing it to him.

It wasn't until I felt certain that he was unknowingly falling into my plot, slowly killing himself. That's I started feeding him later, and later at night.

Making sure it would all lay in his stomach when he went to bed. While making sure that I was already sleeping so that I didn't have to become sexually involved with him.

That was the part of my plan that really hurt me the most. I was destroying my sex life out of spite, and my vendetta against him.

What made it even worse was the fact that I couldn't start going out cheating on me because he was coming home at irregular times of the day complaining that he wasn't feeling good, and I had to be there for Sally during the day.

Beside knowing if I did so. It wouldn't make me any better than him, and I was too far into my plan to start finding fault with myself.

His slow agonizing death was also taking its toll on me, and the more irritated I got the harder it got for me to continue on proceeding with my diabolical plan.

I couldn't count the time that I wanted to reach out and grab hold of him, and literally rape him. That's how frustrated I would get at time.

Then there were times when I had to be a wife to him so I sort of made up for the times I abstained, claiming that I wasn't in the mood, or pretended I was already a sleep, or was too busy to stop what I was doing to oblige him.

If that wasn't enough to discourage him there was always Sally saying to myself.' My God, how could I've used that pour girl the way I doing.' Constantly asking myself. 'Why, and if Tom was worth me involving my own daughter?'

Believe me my revenge wasn't an easy one to undertake. It had a great many regrets along with a lot of traumatic moments.

I still kept telling myself that I loved Tom with all my heart. That I just despised him for cheating on me and continuing on doing so.

Where there was no reason for him to do so other than the fact that he wanted too because he didn't find me desirable anymore.

Up until the time I found out what he was doing I was all over him never denying him anything always catering to his impulsiveness.

Because I was loving it as much as he was just being with him, showing him how much I loved him by doing anything he wanted to for him baring nothing.

I was existing on the haunting thought of him being with some other women most likely saying the same things he was to me while kissing her instant of me.

* * * *

In the matter of a year Tom became sluggishly lazy. His sex drive was diminishing down to 4 times a week, he kept talking about going to see a doctor, but kept putting it off saying he couldn't right now. That there was something he had to finish up first.

All the while this was going on at home, he finally advances to executive manager. Now only working eight, too ten, hours some days and home most evenings unless he was called upon to entertain some potential clients or having to attend an executive meeting.

Otherwise coming home early with me leaving more and more thing for him so snack on like hard boiled eggs injected with bacteria with his beer, and added salt for his eggs.

Surprisingly Tom wasn't showing any signs of gaining any weight, but was he starting to get sagely in a lot of place now.

Twice a week I would go to a Health Spa and vigorously work out doing aerobics. Always making sure to be home before three, in the afternoon when I had to pick up Sally from day care.

I was back to my picturesque self again looking better than I did when I was 17. However, I was always making it a point to check up on Tom's activities by checking up on where he claims to be going.

Especially when he was claiming to be playing golf. Or when he was even claiming to be getting himself involved in playing some tennis, and swimming no less.

Tom never did like sports let alone taking an active part in any of them, but he was doing what he was saying he was doing, that much I knew for sure.

It was at work where I felt certain I had to concentrate my efforts on keeping a close eye on him. I wasn't about to let those other women get very much time with him that was for sure, but it was out of my control if he called and said he had to work late.

I couldn't afford to have him loss his job and robe me of my future earnings. So I couldn't keep checking up on him.

When he would be in an important meeting that might be effecting what little life we did have life together

Lucky for him those activities where the only things keeping him from getting fat and sloppy, but I couldn't help to notice what all that snacking, drinking and eating of my delicious cooking was doing to him. It was starting age him.

I wanted him to get fat and sloppy looking. I never through that what I was doing would age him, and it started to appear on him when he was started getting gray hair, and sort of thin in the face.

That wasn't at all doing what I wanted it to do for him. It was making him look more sophisticatedly mature, and even more appealing too women from what I could see.

I needed to reconfigure my strategy plan. Especially when it came to his gray hair. I was having enough trouble dealing with the women he was already involved with that I knew about I didn't need any more becoming attached to him.

CHAPTER 10

Another year past Sally was 4 years old now I was thirty, looking twenty-five and Tom was thirty-six looking forty-five.

He went to the doctor and the doctor told him to stop eating the greasy foods, cut out salt, and reduce his beer intake.

Also to stop smoking, and to cut down on his sexual activities until he built himself back up again physically.

He wanted to start him on a regimented vitamin plan to being his body back into shape, because he was over exerting himself by trying to do too much.

I was going to make sure that he didn't follow the doctors' orders. By even giving him more physical exercise. That I was sure that I needed more than he did any doctors vitamin plan, and of course.

I was going to have to feed him more for him to keep up his strength. Especially after a good ritualistic bout of having sexual exercise with me. Then only to be appeased by a vigorous delectable snack, just before going to sleep for the night.

After I would see to it that he would roll off me from exhaustion, and would sleep for a good hour. Where upon I would wake him up with something good and nourishing for him to eat to rebuild his strength.

Like a three-day old left over slightly chilled chicken leg that I purposely left sitting out of the refrigerator for three, or four, hours. Before putting it back in the refrigerator to keep cold, so that he would think that it was alright to eat.

By all rights Tom should have died long before his time too, but that man has some sort of biological immunity that just won't stop. Where all I was doing was having an effect on him only physically, and sexually and aging him.

That was the morbid part I didn't like, but I was getting satisfaction from knowing that it wasn't only effecting my sex life but all those other he was having to accommodate, along with me as well, and having to lie to him. Telling him how wonderful it was, or comforting saying.

"That's alright honey it happens to every guy some times. You more so lately considering those stressful days you are having lately having to keep up such a rigorous pace keeping everyone satisfied."

The only satisfaction I was deriving from having to be nurturing to him was knowing that if he wasn't doing it for me. He sure as hell wasn't doing it for any of those other whore's of his.

Watching him deteriorating before my eyes. Knowing that I could stop it. Did seem sadistic, but it wasn't as far as I was concerned.

Tom's drinking became excessive during which he was expressing enraged impulses to strike out at me. He was even becoming belligerent to Sally his own daughter verbally.

Tom changed after he came home from the hospital after being examined. He became sarcastic, verbally abusive, and obnoxiously argumentative not to mention overbearing, and demanding.

It was as if he was being rebellious against me, and even came out and said that he didn't need, want, or love me anymore.

Twice while we were having a disagreement over something petty. He raised his hand to strike me, but stop short of doing so.

Whether he discovered what I was attempting to do to him, or he just wanted out of the marriage once and for all or marriage came to the point that he even approached me suggesting that it might be best if we separated for a while, and actually left me.

During which he came to discover how much it would cost to get a divorce, where he came back home ling to his daughter that he had to go away for a while on company business.

That when my plot really became a battle of survival, rather than one of revenge. Once the bills started to come in. That I had to paid for his extravagant life style living by himself.

It became apparently obvious that what I was doing to him was only half of what he was doing to himself, and where I was concern it was getting easier and easier for me to become unsympathetic towards him.

So that is what prompted Tom too resign himself to coming back home.

When I had no choice but to approach him about his spending and the effect he was having on his daughter's life. Blaming myself not to know how to manage the money for a reason for him to come back home to live out his miscible life.

Which made if all that much easier on me not to feel any pity, or remorse over finishing what I started.

The One thing I was certain about. Was fact that Tom wasn't trusting in anyone including me. Something happened while he was in the hospital and he wasn't telling anyone what it was.

Causing it to become apparently obvious that it wasn't going to be getting any easier for me to carry out my plan. Mainly because I was trying my best to avoid him as much as possible using the excuse that I didn't want him getting mad and hitting me.

Are family life was totally going to hell. The only thing our marriage had going for him more so than me, was the fact that we continued to sleep in the same bedroom together.

As much as I wanted one of my own he wouldn't stand for it.

Saying that if I wanted my own bedroom I was going to have to move out and get a place of my own place to get it.

That there was no way I was going to give him the satisfaction of me moving out of my own home.

Especially with my daughter having to live alone someplace I was totally unfamiliar with. So are marriage going on.

With him up and suddenly going off on a rampage all of his own. Constantly finding fault in everything I did.

Becoming more argumentatively derogatory, and obnoxiously advantageous. Just so he could go storming out of the house too one of his floozies'. As an excuse to come home drunk at 2 or 3 in the morning.

Saying how sorry he was. Affectionately becoming amorous, expecting me to make love to him and eventfully wear me down so that I would make love to himself, using me. Hoping that I would forgive him as I always said I did.

Sex was no longer a pleasurable experience for me. It was becoming a drudgery ordeal of having to force myself to submit to his sexual advances…

Tom never was that sort of man that would use his endowment to obtain personal satisfaction, but what was I to do where I alone was responsible for the changes in him. That were becoming extremely more tormenting on me. Where the effects I was anticipating wasn't happen to him, but the opposite.

Knowing that I was the one who actually created the man he now was becoming. Finding myself actually blaming myself, and feeling guilty about what I did. Wanting to take it all back, and honestly wanting to forget, and forgive his transgression.

It was obvious that I went too far, and he wasn't about to give me the chance to resigned all I was attempting to do too him.

Finding myself hopelessly caught up between what I was attempting to do to him, and blaming myself for the way I failed in my attempt. Which regretfully left me with having to deal with the man I made him into.

He just wouldn't stop his obnoxious demeanor. Even when we were out in public, or at a social gathering. He would purposely embarrass me by making rude innuendos directed towards me.

Once he even had the gall to take me aside to ask me if I would go have sex with his boss. That's how little respect Tom had for me.

That's when I knew that somehow Tom found out about what I was doing to him, and that he knew that I knew, that he was cheating on me.

I don't know how he found out, but he did, and doing what he was doing was telling me that he didn't know how to handle what he found out, and was fighting with himself over refusing to believe that I would do such a thing to him, and was taking his aggravation out on me.

Tom could drink and never show he was drunk, and he never bowed down to anyone, or took their crap.

I couldn't believe that he would have the audacity to even ask me to do such a thing. I got so damn mad. I stormed out of his boss's house, and took a cab home.

Only to have him come home apologizing. Saying how sorry he was, and that it would never happen again.

The man was becoming a Jackal and Hide. I knew what I was doing to him, and he was turning it around, and doing it to me, but in a different way.

That's when my contempt for him grew out of control. As much as I blamed myself over becoming vengeful against him.

I wasn't about to tolerate any more of the way he was retaliating against me, and openly rebelled. Asking for a divorce.

Tom became aggressively more overbearing in his sexual advances towards me. He was cruel, rude, and mocking towards me every chance he could by downgrading my enthusiasm, and showing discontentment.

It was as if he was trying to drive me away from him but I refused to leave demanding that I wasn't, but he was! Even going as far as to say no!

It was a battle of endurance, and he was losing, and that's when the hitting started, and his verbal attacking Sally.

The smacking started, them his hitting on me. When I stepped in to protect Sally having enough of him mocking her.

Using her childish antics as an excuse to strike out at her to get at me. Aimed at me for taking away his authority figure around his house, while attempting to rob him of his manhood.

Using it as an excuse to leave after slapping me across my face, and shoving me back out of his way. Aggressively forcing his way past me. As he went storming out of the house.

Like the fool that I was. Knowing how explosive he was getting, I took him back, for it to happen all over again. Just so I could finish what I started only to hear him openly confess that he had an affair with his secretary at work.

Claiming that when it happened he was so disoriented, confused, and venerable that I was the cause for it to happen.

That it appears that he got her pregnant, but she was willing to go have an abortion. Pathetically saying.

" I just wanted you to know how sorry I am, that it won't happen again, and it's not as if I still don't love you... I love you with all my heart...Please forgive me..."

"Like the stupid gullible fool that I was. Also thinking that now was my chance to make up for what I tried to do to him.

Knowing he wasn't telling me everything, but it was a start for us to come back together again, and he got me to take him back.

Come to find out a mouth later that what Tom told me was only half true. That he spent $10,000 on her during the three, weeks he was gone, and was trying to account for it by saying that he got her pregnant where in fact he was paying her off.

What I didn't find out until after Tom's death was that the man had investments that were worth millions, and here I was thinking only hundreds of thousands, and it was multi-millions.

Also discovering the reason Tom never got fired from the company he worked for, was because he was a major stock holder in it. As well as in a network of health spas, and other company's

I couldn't believe how it was that he manipulated me. By creating arguments, so that he would make it possible to stop giving me his paychecks. So he could cover up all the money he was hiding in safety deposit boxes about the city.

Along with the main reason he stops his divorce proceeding, and came back with his tail between his legs.

It was all a big cover up. Because he didn't want me to find out what he was really worth, and here I thought it was because he found out about what I attempting to do to him.

That bastard played me just so he could keep his life style going the way he had it going for him. Getting me to accept him back into the house, not caring about my feelings towards him, or his for me.

The nearest I could figure was that he wasn't only paying me, but those other women he was involved with as well.

Or that things weren't going as good as I imagined they were supposed to be going between all of them sexually.

I know if they were getting the same I was getting they sure as hell would want to get rid of him, where I was the unfortunate one who was still married to him.

Before Tom's death sexually things were going from bad to worse between us. All that attentive care I devoted to catering to him was doing its job better than I thought it was.

* * *

In the years prior to Toms death are sex life became so pathetic that it wasn't even worth the effort of me taking off my pants anymore for.

He became inconsiderate, selfish, and impudently unless. He was either half crooked from alcohol or beer, or so tanked up to where he became a perverted demented bastard demanding, or taking what he felt like taking.

Not caring how much it hurt me, or what satisfaction he derived out of it. He just took and I'd to put out or lose out, and I was getting so close so I did what he wanted and I gritted my teeth and lied to him.

I didn't have him, he had me where the only resource that was open to me was to submit, or leave and lose out on everything before I could legally get to any of it, or maybe having all he needed to put me behind bars for attempting to murder him.

Tom was no longer the man I loved and married. He was a decrepit, despicable drunken slob of a man who deserved what he got.

Thank God for bad fish. That's what finally got him after making Tom begged, pleaded and crawl on his hands and knees for me to take him to the hospital.

Where I waited for a good two, hours making sure that he was dead before calling an ambulance to take him to the hospital.

Tom died at the age 37 in November 1975 when Sally was 5. On that very day. All the turmoil, chaos, and previous hassles settled down into a somewhat a livable environment.

No longer having to be subjected to being ignored, or having to put up with his atrocities where sex, and my standard of living was concern.

At least it wasn't anything like it was when he was alive. Having to put up with his obnoxiously reprehensible attitude, while listening to him talking in a polite obnoxious tone of voice while implying the opposite of what he was saying most of what he was saying was nothing but lies.

When I no longer had to be cooking him those special meals of his damn pork chops cooked medium raw injected to a middle dose of toxic marinate, or those damn bagels of his with lot's, and lots of spreadable ever so delectable creamy cheese, and his chilly with two, day old hamburger, or his ever so delectable baked beans with all that yummy big chunks of ham with special additives of my own making, plus of course lot's, and lots of salt.

※ ※ ※ ※

Before Tom's tragic death I was back again being the loving catering wife back to catering too my loving husbands every whim. Just waiting for him to thank me by dying.

I must admit his ferocious appetite really kept me hoping… I could hear him saying when he got sick, and started throwing up." Honey this tastes bad."

Where I would simply blame it on the beer, or when he would ask." Honey this chicken is tasting bad." I would have replied back." Just eat it. I wouldn't give it to you if it was bad"

I can remember as if it was just happening. When he would come home and head straight for the refrigerator. Where I would always make sure what was in it was greasy, or bad, or damn close to it.

Keeping what I was feeding Sally and myself in a separate refrigerator down in the basement when we most of the time eat before he got home, or after he left to go to work

Tom was trying to turn back the clock 10 years where I was trying to speed it up 20 or 30. Ahead of his time.

While he was using his charm, and passive seductive manner of congeniality attempting to pray on my none existing love for him. Where far too much was already said and done.

I put myself though too much hardship and emotional mental anguish to fall back in love with him all over again.

Loving him once got us where we were. I wasn't going to take the chance that he would me put through it again.

That not only went for Tom. It went for any man as far as I was concern. As far as men were concerned. They weren't even good for sex. Let alone wasting my time living with.

Find them, seduce them, and leave them with longing for more. Was going to be my motto. Then only if they were rich enough to be able to afford the honor of me letting them get to me, and then only when I wanted them too.

I admit, but only to myself that I might have been cheating on him some myself. Strictly out of desperation you understand.

He didn't want to have anything to do with me when I thought I was pregnant. So I prayed on it a lot just too relieve the stress and tension I was under.

I might have had myself a few insignificant flirtations myself, but Tom was continuously carrying on affairs with other women as well and I only sought it fair to do likewise to him.

Besides golf, and tennis lessons didn't come cheap and I was stashing the money I was supposedly paying for them.

Thinking that Tom's insurance wasn't going to keep me in the glamorous life style I was now accustomed too, and I had Sally my daughter's future to think about.

I had to scheme and connive with the expenses to insure that my daughter and I would make it through the hard times.

I would by things on credit using my credit card, and hold what I bought for two days. When I would take them back and get the money back. Making sure it would show up on my charge, but not the refund on my monthly statement.

Then when it did I explained it to Tom as an over charge, and he never thought anything about it after that. Seeing how he was now getting himself involved in the household expenses.

Tom never quarreled about me buying risqué outfit that accentuated my feathers, or looked very sexy on me.

In fact, he never really questioned anything I bought. When I just wanted to have some extra spending money to spend on whatever I wanted to. So I could stash away for the rainy days that were going to be coming up.

In one year I accumulated over $30,000 and was investing the money in stocks and investments of my own.

Where I couldn't have done it if I paid for the few pleasures I was getting out of my miscible life and besides I needed a sexual outlet myself...

I mean what harm could any guy possibly do? They couldn't get me pregnant that's for damn sure.

As for becoming emotionally attached. The furthest thing I was wanting to get myself involved emotionally with was with any guy.

I was having too much trouble getting rid of the one I already had. To want to concern myself with another one.

I was being socially discreet and never gave anyone a reason to gossip about me, or my moral character.

I kept my affairs distant from where I lived so that anyone who knew me would think of me as the motto wife, and contributor to Tom success.

I made it a point to be where they weren't, amongst my class of people top which I never belonged with that upper class of people to begin with.

Where I felt most comfortable is where no one knew me, or anything about my life to those I fraternized with.

I said nothing unless they pried it out of me, and then only enough to let those busy body meddling snobs use their imagination.

Where in reality I was a women living with an arrogant drunk making myself out the one who was sacrificing everything towards her husband success.

I was known as Donna Storm the good time girl who wasn't easy to get to. I wore a wig, and wide rimmed glasses, and was out to have a good

Who wanted the man that I was going to be seen with to put all he had forth to impress me, and not to just to inflate his macho egotistical...

Then I said politely. "Thanks you for an enjoyable evening, or time. If you are here when I come back, I would be happy to see you again." Them leave always leaving them wanting more of nothing they never got.

Always making it a point to pay for myself so they never felt cheated taking a cab when I would leave having it come to the front door of where I was at just in case,

My double life was exhausting at time, but I set my goals high to keep it exhausting. My life with Tom while he was alive had to appear tediously exhausting, and I couldn't let it disrupt my previous already glamorous life style.

I didn't want to draw any suspicion to my intentions. Not even from my daughter. Even before Tom's death when Tom was starting to show signs of him becoming weaker and weaker.

Even when he knew something was definitely wrong, and kept going to the doctor. Where the doctor kept telling him to lay off the carbohydrates, and the greasy foods he was still relying on me to feed and tend to him.

I had to make certain that he wouldn't suspect me as the culprit behind what was happening to him where he had no one else that would care for him that he didn't have to pay to do so.

Where I insisted to be the only cook in the entire household, and only allowing a twice a week maid to come in to help me keep the house looking lived in.

I wanted my freedom to manage my own household and be free when I wanted to be after Tom left, and before he was to come home, and taking Sally to a special day care during the day.

So I could always manage the way to keep getting him to eat what I fed him, and drinking his beer, and to make sure to kept his smoking habit going where he was up to a good two and a half packs per day increasing daily. Thanks to my efforts of keeping him healthy.

All the while I kept assuring him that the doctor didn't know what he was talking about. That he was living as healthy as I was, saying.

"Look at me I'm eating the same things you're, and there's nothing wrong with me. Your just worn down somewhat that's all by letting your job get to you.

You need to say home more so that I can take better care of you, and where I can be around when you want to relax in my loving arms...

Oh, my... You see I know what's good for you. I must say you sure are feeling very amorously healthy today I must say...

Now I don't want you to worry about anything and just let me handle you just like I always have been doing.

I know what's best for you at times like this. This is why I devoted so much time and effort in making sure that you enjoy my cooking.

I don't know why the doctor is telling you that what I'm doing for you isn't good for you are as healthy as when I first met you, and you're not a young guy anymore, and you're still are as strong as you ever were. Somewhat sluggish, but that's only to be expected."

That damn doctor Tom started to go too. Got him into starting to jog. I didn't like that so I made a relentless effort to keep him humping tired. Like it or not he wasn't going to neglect me.

He could do his jogging afterwards, then only after he had himself a good stable breakfast.

I wasn't about to deprive myself so he could go gallivanting off exerting himself and neglecting me.

I was entitled as his wife to certain benefits, and I was going to make sure that I was going to get them. If I was going to be the one to have to care for me. As any good attentive wife would tell you. She has to be flexible in order to accommodate his urges.

I would be dammed if I was going to let him reap all the rewards of his husbandry, and deprive myself what was rightfully and legally mine to receive when the mood strikes me.

At least until I was able to implement phrase three. Where it took some time, and a considerable amount of energy on his part to exert the last of what was left of all he could give. Jealousy making sure to deprive those whores of his of getting any satisfaction out of him.

Following the principle of any good house wife. Making sure that he takes care of her first. Making sure he'll be in no condition to go elsewhere for what he gets more than he can handle at home.

Waking Tom up around 5 AM was usually the way he loved to start his day off. His rigorous schedule consisted of keeping me up from 5 AM. Which morally took too around 6:00 before taking his shower. Then down too breakfast around 6:30 and off to work about 9 AM.

The mornings were always his peak times. He got rather sluggish in the evenings, and kept his sexual activities down to about two, times a week at night time. Just before going to sleep.

He was in a routine that I established for him, and it was gruelingly killing him, if he was doing any carousing he was going to be doing it on his days off in the evenings.

That kept alternating upon when the urge strikes me. As for the early morning I made sure make them rigorously exhausting spastically usually four, times a week.

Tom was fading gradually. On three, occasions he had to go to the hospital for dehydration, or his cholesterol count was exceeding the danger limit, or for vitamin deficiency where he developed diabetes.

His blood was thickening, and developing clouts his arteries, and he was developing internal cysts under his skin, and his blood pressure was high and getting higher.

The doctor kept saying diet, exercise, and for him to change his living habits. So now that they were monitoring him more closely I had to change me tactics.

I dropped the greasy food, and switched to ice cream. The creamy kind with more salt added. Concentrating on keeping them smooth, and delicious by adding chocolate, or strawberry syrup which he couldn't get enough

But continuously kept up, actually increasing his intake of bad baked pork chops, slow cooked corn beef... steaks, and ham with mashed potatoes.

Along with lots of gravy made form only the best grease. Making him believe that I boiled, or baked everything of course.

I even cut down his daily intake of eggs, but replaced it with sweet rolls with added butter with rolls filled with nuts. The good things for him to eat.

Plus, seeing how he was getting so healthy from joying I even throw in more strenuous morning sex, and less relaxation time. I wanted him up and out of the home doing what the doctor told him, and of course his manly thing with his other ladies in his life.

Tom wasn't stupid by any means. I had to be sneaky and conniving as hell not to mention manipulative.

I was never quit sure where Tom was coming form. There was no telling when he might lash out at me again, or just how far, or how long I could chance to deceive him.

Keeping him from asking himself why I was catering up to him, and why I continued to be a wife to him. With the doctors obviously warned him repeatedly that his health was deteriorating, but for some reason he just excepted thing as they were, and that's what worried me the most.

Knowing Tom was a killer once, and he wouldn't hesitate to become one again. It was nerve-racking-to say the least. Not knowing what was going on in that devious mind of his.

Knowing what love he did have left for me was hanging on a thread. Just waiting to break and I would be the one being put in a box instead of him.

I didn't know if he was wantonly excepting what I was doing, or just waiting for the right moment too end it once and for all. Keeping me on edge all the time wanting to stop, but fearing if I did, and he really found out what I was doing to him. It would all over for me for sure.

I would run into Nancy once in a while at the spa I was going too. She just as much as told me that Tom was on the verge of leaving his wife, and as for his would be girlfriends all, but one has just as much moved on in their lives.

That the one named Janet was still hanging around where the others all still see Tom, but only on rear occasions and all moving on into different lives, or careers with Tom's blessing no less.

That meant that it was primarily just Nancy and the one named Janet where Nancy was convinced that Tom was working on getting rid of her, so that it would only be just Tom and her.

Nancy still never did catch on that she was talking to Tom's wife when she was talking to me.

One would think that she would have gotten curious, and at least found out what her competition looked like, but just by looking at her I could see why she wasn't concerned about me.

Even after I was grueling working out three, times a week, she was still looking far better than me, and if that wasn't bad enough. Her damn tits even got bigger, and firmer than mine were.

You know how us women always develop that little stomach pouch just above our pelvic mound that plumes out up to our waist. Not her.

Herr's was as flat as flat could get, so flat in fact that she was still showing that pelvic bulge protruding out from her pelvic area out from beneath her stretch pants.

She was really starting to piss me off...! And the way she talked about how Tom was hitting on her nonstop, and the way she looked in that exercise body suit would make a one eye blind guy lust for her.

Her damn thighs were still firmer than mine were. Even after taking all that damn pounding going on between them.

Where mine was sort of flabby in spots where all the pounding was going on. You know just below the cleaves of the butt cheeks where everything had been stretched out of proportion from having kids.

Developing that crease, or indentation between where the thighs stopped, and the sagging butt cheeks lapped over. Was totally none existent where see was concern.

How I was really wanting to tear her eyes out of their sockets, and literally deflate those damn tits of hers. So that they would cave inwards towards her chest.

All I could think about was ways to make her look ugly, and grotesque looking. I just know that after I was finished with Tom. S was going to be my next victim... I wasn't about to let her get away with being better than me. That was for damn sure.

All the way home I couldn't stop thinking about what I was going to do to get back at that damn bitch! I mean I was looking sensational at a teenager and no matter how hard I tired there was no way I could ever regain the exquisiteness that I once was. There she was just as old as I was looking like a virgin teenager.

Hating her even more because she was the one who started the whole thing between Tom and I, but the second I got out of the car and walked back into the house.

My mind instinctively went back onto Tom and my concerns about him finding out about what I was up to. Thinking to myself one again.

'If he ever so much as suspected that I was out to kill him. How he wouldn't hesitate to kill me first for sure.'

Knowing that Tom wanted out of the marriage, but he couldn't seem to break free from me. I guess in his own morbid way; he really did love me.

That in his mind he knew he was doing wrong, but justifying it by thinking that he was giving me everything.

It really disturbed me to think after all I've doing to him he was just thinking of me as still number one on his pedestal, and that he was still feeling certain that he could trust me.

Thinking that I was the only person he would never have to suspect to be the one who would attack him with the intent of killing him, especially with food of all things.

I mean I was eating the same things he was, and I wouldn't be feeding him anything bad knowing that it was.

All a person would have to do is too condition their system slowly to tolerate the transition of accepting bad from good food with someone mixing it with additional additives. That were, meant to attack one's vital organs, and arteries and still go about undetectable through moral bodily functions, but where Tom was concern it was actually working out that way, or was it?

That's what concerned me the most where Tom was concern where I was going to have to wait patiently for the way I was attempting to kill was going to have to take its course.

Of course food poison would show up in his blood, but so would everything else. They couldn't blame anyone, but himself for eating bad food, and if I wasn't there to help him. They would have to declare it an accident by accidental food poisoning.

Especially if the culprit was bad fish to be the means of his demise. So that everything else would be overlooked, or contributed to what was in the bad fish.

With the added list of other conditions that he was constantly warned about contributing to his cause of death.

The key too being successful was using his own vises against him, and patronizingly fraternizing his fondness for how enjoyable they are when he eats them.

While staying oblivious to what his doctor was advising him to do, saying. "Why didn't someone tell me what was going on with him? He never mentions that there was anything seriously for me to be concerned about.

I was always telling him. Making him deserving of his own fate so he can never turn to you and say." What are you trying to do kill me...?"

Not excepting any blame for his bullheadedness. Using his own abstinence against himself. Making his rebellious nature be the cause behind denouncing one's advice in spite of himself.

That when one can come back at him and say. "No way could I ever kill you. Your too damn bullheadedly stubborn to ever listen to me...

Or say I can't see how the food could had been bad. I ate the same thing he did, and I wasn't being effected the way he was...

Using ignorance and luck of the Irish as one's only excuse that I didn't suffer the same fate that he did. Would exonerate me of any wrongdoing.

The main thing was to keep them thinking that it was their stupidity not yours. Lose that innocence and you might as well forget it, and try something else more direct.

I would always keep bugging Tom to get involved in doing more exercising, trying to keep him physically fit and healthy for him.

It was my way of finding out how Tom was feeling physically as well as energetically. While always making a point to flaunt myself, and of course always serving up an extra treat afterwards as my way of expressing how happy he made me.

The way I saw it was. Give any man enough encouragement to get himself a quickly, and if he doesn't jump at the chance.

There's a likelihood that he'll want to go after it, but doesn't have the energy to go after it. The more he abstains the more the possibility will be that your plan is working, or he's cheating on you.

"When they say." Not today honey, or I haven't the time. That's the time to move in, and get them interested in doing the one thing you want them to do.

My idea behind it. Was to drain him of his energy so that he'll want more to eat of my good food.

Making the sex strenuous, not letting him be too anxious to get his. By making him work hard for what he wants, and don't let him off easy. I loved making Tom sweat. When he falters that's not alright.

By not letting him get away without not giving me what I want out of him

Like it, or not going at it again, and again.

Until he at least comes close to being the guy you once married, and not just let him roll over, and ignore me.

As a woman you got what even man wants. One just have to convince him that he wants it, and I already done that. By making myself more available outside the bedroom, that's the key I used.

Don't let him anywhere near a bed, and if they want to end it quick I force him by using what makes him a man. Too want more by stimulating him visually, and by prolonging his impulsiveness to have it.

I personally went and had myself some coaching as to how to delay the inevitable and how to inflate his other brain desire. The key is visual.

Let him watch and feel while you inspire the insatiable desire and holding him back from being to eagerly submissive by cutting you short.

I had to learn he very thing I always had where Tom was concern. Tom could never restrain himself to day no, to me. The thought alone was all he needed to insight his lustful desire for me.

I agree not all men are into longevity. Where the longer I kept him exhausting himself not for him to get what he wants, but me if he wanted me to stop so that he could rest.

The more he would the more I would feed him my good food as he would kick back letting himself back with a full gut full of all those additives I added extra to the snacks I would give him in it.

I admit it's a slow tedious process but it was working. Well at least I thought it was. Even his own doctor didn't contest the autopsy report when he came out saying." Well I kept warning him and he wouldn't listen…"

I found that wearing short skirts and red underpants was the most effective form of intimidation to get him motivated.

Especially when those infamous words would come up." Honey I'm not really in the mood right now."

I didn't feel sorry for him or let in intimidate me by his rejections of your suggestiveness, but yet let him become inspired by a little motivation.

By giving him a peek-a-boobs of what I was wearing under that short skit. While nonchalantly moving closer and closer to him. Letting his manly imagination work it's inspiring magic to do the rest, and once I had in attention I didn't let him go until I exhaust him totally.

Believe me I was doing myself a favor if nothing else, by increasing his longevity, and when that happens all I had to do afterwards was to feed him twice as much.

I didn't just give in and allowed myself to lose out on any golden opportunely that most likely only comes around when I wanted it to.

I stayed in control, and don't let him get off easy... Once I had his adrenaline going, and his heart pumping and got him striving for the want of me, and not thinking about anything else.

I used him to drain every ounce of energy out of himself to where I would have to feed him to regain some of it back.

I was being the women I was born to be by enticing, and taunting him. By letting him get close but, not so close that he'll see, or touch too much. Smelling provocative intoxicating and seductively enchanting.

Even through he's seen, and been there before. Captivating him as if it was his first time, worked for me.

With Tom the more he struggles to retrains himself the hungrier he became afterwards. My plan was working mainly because Tom was always a one women man even though there were others in his life he was venerable in every way to me.

My plan was a five year one. I did it in a little over three, and Tom was as strong as a bull. All one need is the right ingredients to make him keep on coming back for more.

As distasteful as it might appear, and it's not as if doing something distasteful is all the offensive to us women. What's that old saying about a women being scorn. When having to tolerate being scorn?

Believe me I get over it when finally, all your efforts were finally realized. The simple truth was that I knew Tom's sexual appetite, and I used it to my advantage for my benefit and to deprive others of depriving me.

Being a wife, or just someone who happens to be in love with him. You should also be aware of their sexual appetite, and it's not above us women to create an additional desire. Just to develop a way to monitor his faithfulness.

Any added effort could be beneficial in the long run no matter the reason behind you might be suspicious of him.

It's like investing in the stock market. It's always the long term investment that finally pay off not the short term ones when others are also invested in the same stock.

Like when I feed Tom late at night, and he went to bed on a full stomach. I would make sure that my hands were resting on his hip, right beside you know what?

In no time at all Tom was exhibiting an urge that he couldn't suppress anymore, and afterwards I made it a point to find him something to eat before he went to sleep. As for the eating. The means justifies the end result.

There's always a way to motivate. It's just a matter if you want to, or not, but I knew when I started my plan. That once I started turning back wasn't going to be an option.

I suppose there was always divorcing him. Even though that is an option to consider. I guess it all depends on how bad your situation is, or what you hope to benefit from whatever time, and abuse you put into the relationship.

In order for one to know how far one will go to get some form of satisfaction out of all she sacrificed for during the marriage, or relationship.

Like I said before. It took me a little over three years, to achieve my vendetta. During which I endured a great deal anxiety, doubts, and apprehensions but, I also gained immensely by the knowledge that no one else got him, and I got what was rightfully mine. All of it.

Along with the personal satisfaction that I was the better of the best. Of all the women he became involved with

DISPLACEMENT INTENT

✳ ✳ ✳ ✳

I was thirty-five years old when Tom died with a whole new life ahead of me, and all the time in the world to enjoy it with million to ingratiate myself with.

I still had my looks, and the memories of are first wonderful years we spent together, and of curse Sally.

Looking back on it all Tom did have a good life in all respects. Other than making a pig out of himself by indulging himself with other women, and of course where my home cooking, and sweets were concerned.

At Tom's funeral I counted a total of seven, women including the three, I saw with Nancy at the hospital. Along with the satisfaction of finally meeting Nancy openly face to face.

Where she practically fainted when she found out who I was. She was so damn panic stricken. It was all she could do from stopping from pissing in her pants. That's how shocked she was.

When I walked up and stood before the platform where Tom's body was lying in a casket, staring directly at her. As she sat in the first roll along with her other three, friends all staring at me.

Nancy rose up with her hands covering most of her face with her chin dropping down onto the floor between her legs. Being followed by her three, friends rising up too hurriedly walk Nancy out of the funeral pallor.

I didn't know, nor did I even bother to ask who the other women were to him. As I stood watching them leaving one by one without saying a word to me.

Until all that was left was a small group of some that I knew and a lot that I didn't. Along with my daughter Sally and I watching all those women leaving.

With I standing as Tom's vindicated wife, and murderess who had it all, where all those others women had was nothing, but the time they wasted themselves a man who screwed them more than he did me.

With the credibility of being a loving devoted wife. Being shown sympathy over her lose by his friends and business associates.

I won but at the cost of only losing a man who I lost all love for. Tom's memory will be his epitaph to constantly remind me what love could really do to a person.

There would never be another Tom. His life and accomplishments touched many, but was only shared by one. Where his one and only true love was his daughter Sally

CHAPTER 11

After Tom's death I never remarried. I sold the house and bought another hoping to forget, but there was no forgetting Tom.

As much as I grieved over what I did too Tom. I knew in my heart it was the only way to truly end things between us.

Knowing Tom couldn't live without me, and I couldn't bare living with him any longer than I already did.

I knew what it was that was making him be the way he was towards me. It wasn't the other women, or because of his celibacy during my pregnancies that was totally self-inflicted.

It was due to his past life. That's all he could ever think about. He struck out at me because I made him into the upstanding person he didn't want to be.

Tom was one who loved living on the edge. He was his own achiever, and highly recognized as well as respected out of fear for what he was recognized for being so good at.

I have admitted what he accomplished did make a new life for us, and he did it totally on his own. Mainly because it was a challenge to him, but once the challenge was gone, his past exploits became his haunting aspirations.

For years he strived to show me how much he loved me struggling to become someone he wasn't because he wanted me to have everything.

Using me as his driving force as well as his status symbol that he presented proudly always before his benefactors and amongst his peers. Seeing to it that I got the respect and admiration deserving of me being the one he loved.

Then when he believed that killed he his son. No matter what anyone tried to tell him he never stopped blaming himself for his son's death.

Tom was a man entrapped wanting to revert back with only one thing standing in his way. "Me."

His dependency on me doubled as he sought to redeem himself for killing his son as well as using it for an excuse for reverting back to living the life style that he relished thrived in. Living by using his brains instead of his brawn.

By secretly sneaking around behind my back and getting away with attempting to rekindle a renewed recognition that he so desperately needed to reveal in.

Deceiving himself that it was to make a better life for himself as well as me, and was getting away with pulling it off. Until I overheard Nancy talking amongst those three, other women while in the hospital.

Then when I became pregnant again Tom felt renewed rejuvenating ambitions. Once again concentrating his life around his child, but also knowing that he was doing and wanting to continue things that he was already too involved in to instantly back out.

That he was going to have to do so vicariously to insure that his child would never have to go through what he did because he felt insecure about him not making enough working in substandard positions that he couldn't see to get above, and was bettering himself working around his limited position.

Then when I miscarried again all his inhabitation dropped back onto me. That's when Nancy really got a foot hold into my marriage and I became the obstacle where she was concern.

It was through her that Tom was able to revert back into his previous life of crime. When the sex started Tom didn't look on it as cheating on me, but as a means of escaping the bonds that I was inhibiting him from pursuing.

It never once occurred to me just how badly my miscarrying was effecting him. Mainly because Tom really never confided in my all that much about a lot that transpired during his childhood and what I did find out was so tragic.

I didn't want to hear about it, but unfortunately little by little what I was finding out I was at the same time trying to block it out of my mind and I only tried to concentrate on what could affect me that I concerned myself about.

Tom was the sort of person one didn't want to learn to much about. Mainly because the more one heard the more horrid they became over discovering what type of person he really was.

I came to discover one of Tom's constant fears he was living under during my pregnancy.

DISPLACEMENT INTENT

Was prompted by seeing his own mother having a miscarriage trying to give birth too, twins. When he was only six, years old, and the horrors of what he witnessed haunted him constantly.

Which became his most intolerable fear. Picturing her giving birth to two dead under developed babies plagued him where I was concern. Not wanting the same thing to happen to his child.

Tom needed that release of having intercourse. Because if I can believe what he told me about his life.

It was because that was the way he was taught to believe is to be the only way to totally satisfy a woman sexually, and not to do it until she was totally satisfied sexually. For it to be his way of expressing his admiration for the women he was sharing himself with.

I couldn't believe it when he told me. That his first sexual experience was with a grown woman when he was 8 years old.

When he told me my first thought was. "No way...!" I had three brothers I knew better, but the way he describes it.

It didn't matter to the women all she wanted was someone to pay attention to her. Because her boyfriend went off with one of the other women in the motorcycle gang she was traveling with. Where Tom's sister was also one of the girls in the gang who was dating the leader of the gang. Who took a liking to Tom dragged him along with the gang at times? Having him sit on the handle bars of his bike as the gang's mascot.

Tom really didn't share a sexual experience physically, as well as emotionally. Until he was twelve, where he was taught extensively by one particular adult women, and established his concept behind finishing with intercourse.

I was no expert when it came to judging him. All I could attest to was what I personally experienced when I was with him. And only had a few affairs to be able to judge him against them.

It takes any very long to determine the level of satisfaction I received to realize that the way Tom knew how to stimulate all the right places to figure out that only a woman who knew how to appease a woman could have taught him.

Even though he was repetitious it never was the same way twice. His ritualistic way was mind boggling to say the least. At least where I was concern, and eventually was also having the same effect on those other women as well.

His abstaining was making a nervous-wreck out of him, and he needed to be made love too, not just one to have sex with.

He absorbed something from the interaction and even more so from intercourse that very few men that I knew did.

It was his means of unleashing his bottled up emotions. Form the internal sensations of the bonding together.

To him it was the ultimate moment. That gave making love the importance that it so richly deserved, that made it so meaningful.

Tom had this propensity of getting his point across when he wasn't able to achieve his ultimate goal. He became amorously frustrated and vigorously motivated to drive himself harder.

I often asked him what made him obsess so violently. His reply was. "A man and women were meant to be joined in a common bond of unity. The act is meaningless unless that bond is achieved.

Man has no business sharing or bestowing himself within the inner-sanction of a women most precious gift that God himself blessed her with.

That doing so was meant for man, as well as for the women to ravel in the revelations of their unity. That comes from within the shared serenity of the union itself. As self-righteous as it sounds it is my way.

I'm not a religious man but I do believe the woman is Gods most precious gift he could have ever bestowed upon man.

Whereas otherwise they hold no other position over man. They're just as everyone else, with certain exceptions you understand that should be respected by man, or at least by me I see do difference. If they strike me I will do so right back as I would a man who would dare to do so."

I could understand what those other women found so desirable in Tom. He was a man with principles, who held women in high esteem where they should be recognized highly.

Once any women become associated with his ideals. It does become an obsession to experience more out of curiosity if nothing else.

DISPLACEMENT INTENT

If in fact he can be believed, and that's when he becomes an addiction, and that's that I strongly believe what made him so damn special to them, knowing that setting everything else aside he did for me.

Once one gets close to him he does becomes a totally different person. The difference between those other women, and myself. Is that I stopped caring, and they needed him to never stop carrying about them.

Their lives became dependent on me not becoming disenchanted with them. Where I just need to tolerate him.

I knew all too well what I had to do. There were sides to Tom that on one knew accept for me. As reprehensible as my action seemed.

Tom wasn't as terrible as I describe him. I just made sure I didn't provoke him to expose the side of him that only I knew about. Until it finally dawned on me that what I did for him, was what he couldn't do for himself.

Tom lived a tormented life never being able to sleep through the night. Always waking up swinging, shouting, or sweating profusely from the nightmare that haunted him over the horrible things he's done, and had to endure in his life.

I never ventured to pry into his past, but I was the one who had to hold, and comfort him while he convulsively trembled in my arms.

Tom has a nasty disposition added to an already violent temper and then combine with the environment in which he lived.

Always having to live in constant fear that he himself might become victimized by those he has to rely upon. Like that incident in Iowa where he was nearly killed himself, because he believed in those who sent him into almost certain death.

Neither Tom or I were deceiving ourselves. Knowing how deeply involved he was in the syndicate. That those who trusted him weren't out looking for him, and what could, and will happen to the both of us when they did find out.

That in itself never stopped haunting the both of us, but mostly me. Knowing Tom's train of thought regarding defensive mind training self-preservation.

Even though Tom did a damn good job of hiding our identity there was always that change that someone might recognize him.

Has much as I hated to admit it I knew why Tom was using those bitches the way he was. He couldn't risk exposing himself so he was having them doing it for him.

Tom was good at everything he did I'll say that for him. He used any means, or anyone to do what he had to do, and he took sadistic pleasure in being the one to do it himself, but the one thing he couldn't do for himself was to put himself out of his own misery

He never bragged or apologized to anyone for anything. He manipulates and expedited where everyone else was concern, and that also even including me, and his own daughter as well.

When it came to doing something that has to be done. He did it himself. Only having himself to account for what he did, and not having to concern himself over someone else holding anything over him.

No one knew Tom better than I, and I didn't even know him as well as I thought I did. Basically because I stopped wanting to notice what was going on with him, but what I did know, and didn't really take all that much time in trying to recognize.

Was his moods, and his actions that I should have been taking an interest in. Such as when he would resent himself over something he did, or couldn't undo.

Nancy thought she saw him for what he was, but she was in love with him, and like me, found excuses for his actions, and those she couldn't. She forgot, or blamed herself for ignoring.

She was right on one score, she was becoming more compatible with Tom than I was, but Tom wasn't going to let her, or anyone else get close to him. Too where they could get at him to do him any harm.

Tom had to be in authority. His ignorance was a facade to cleverly conceal his ulterior motives. That man had no heart, or concern, or regard for anyone besides himself and I.

People were terrified of Tom even his own co-workers. That's why Nancy became involved with him.

The two, of them were using each other to protect each other. While orchestrating criminal acts to gain from.

DISPLACEMENT INTENT

* * * *

The story Tom told me about what happened at work one day. Found its way back into my mind, and for some reason I started recalling what he told me. When we were having dinner one night.

He told me that one of Tom's supervisors was reprimanding a friend of his for something that someone else did, and the guy stood and took it. Allowing himself to be embarrassed in front of the rest of his co-workers.

The next day that supervisor was walking from his car to work. When his friend came speeding around the corner of a building, where the supervisor was walking in the same direction towards him

Where luckily his friend. Stopped short. In front of the supervisor in fact, within only inches from actually hitting him.

Tom said. That the guy got out and stood beside his car. When another co-worker walked past them, and heard him saying to his boss. Who was standing shaking profusely in front of the car.

" Shit...! Sorry boss. It's a good thing this old caddy had good brakes, but who knows when they could fail...? I guess that's what insurance if for. I guess you got lucky this time. You best be more careful in the future if I were you." Then he got back in his car and drove off.

Tom couldn't help to elaborate on what his co-worker claimed he witnessed. So much so I knew it was him he was talking about, even before he said.

"Now that's how life threatening life can be. When one Fuchs with someone who you think is beneath you. One best watch their ass. They could wind up kissing it in a way they could never imagine."

Tom made his point about his co-worker demonstrating how lucky that supervisor was that his friend stopped in time. Or he would must assuredly have his ass shoved up into his obnoxious big mouth.

Tom then went on to elaborate on the incident, saying that after that incident. That supervisor did everything he could to kiss his friend's ass. Knowing how close he came to being killed if his friend wouldn't have stopped in time. Realizing just how lucky he was to have lived through it.

Tom had this way about him. That everyone noticed, and the last thing anyone wanted to do was to go up against him or get on his bad side.

Tom would hold marshal art, classes during lunch. Showing everyone at work what he was capable of doing if he was provoked, by putting on demonstrations. For the sole purpose of inciting intimidation amongst his peers.

When Tom wanted a raise he would ask for it, and eventually got it. If he didn't strange terrifying things began to happen to the supervisor, or his family that he asked to get the raise from.

The same thing went for when Tom felt himself ready for a promotion he would go to his superior, and ask for one.

Once he came home, and told me that he was turned down for a promotion that he felt he was more qualified for than the guy who got it.

Not more than four, weeks later. His present supervisor quits recommending Tom for his position.

Nothing could be linked to Tom, but it seems that his supervisor's wife and is 14-year-old daughter disappeared for several days, and when they returned. After which Tom's supervisor had already quit and appointed Tom to his position.

From there on it was only a matter of stepping up the ladder of success for Tom while appointing his replacement to fill his previous position. Which of course was Nancy

For someone like Tom with a limited education to be in the position of a unit manager making major decision. Seemed a bit peculiar, but knowing Tom the way I did. I knew better than to under estimate him.

If one stops to think about his mistresses, and the positions they were being placed in. It would kind of give one a picture of what Tom was doing.

Then assume how it was that he managed to be in the position to be there for them. When they needed someone to support, and see them through rough times.

Where I thought was in the company he was working at. Coming to find out that wasn't the case. They were being place in other companies.

That it was how he was able to learn what he needed to know about the activities of upper associates within not only his company, but others as well.

DISPLACEMENT INTENT

Where he used his influence to place them in the positions of knowing who's, who within the companies, and obtaining access to what those women were getting for him.

So he could blackmail figure heads, and high ranking officials within certain firms, and even some outside the firms like city officials.

Like the one he finally got the one named Janet into. He had her working for a financial investment firm as a private secretary to one of the board members.

He was using everyone, and I nerve had any idea what he was doing behind my back thinking only about the fact that he was cheating on me.

I never know how much money Tom was worth until all his financial advisers started contacting me, and the banks making contact with me.

Asking me about what I wanted to do with his safe deposit boxes, and when I went to see what was in them.

I couldn't believe all that he had on different people. Pictures, documents, tapes you name it he had it.

Everyone who was involved with Tom knew that sticking with him was a smart move on their part.

Then to find out what he was doing with his share of the money he was getting. Was investing it in companies that Janet was supplying him with the names.

That were what were considered dormant companies, but were soon, or on the verge of making it big, or were just hanging out there blousing back and forth. Using his influence, he got them to tip one way or the other. Buying in cheap and selling high.

There could had been more than I didn't find out about, but as far as I knew Tom had seven, women working for him in different companies, and was accumulating more with each company he got involved with.

Once Tom had Nancy promoted to assistant vice president Tom gained almost total control of the company he was working for.

Using her he got only the best of the high priced call girls to be invited at his get together. To be arm candy for company executives and city officials.

In order to get those girls to those executives into compromising situations with them, and from what I could figure.

Business, and social gatherings meant the glamor and prestige that I always wanted to be a part of.

I never paid much attention to what really went on while attending them. I just loved the socializing with prominent figures of the elite society, and people in high positions.

A lot of the women I met there. I thought to be the wives of the men they came with, but Tom enlightened me too the fact. That most of them were call girls being paid to be seem with them. More for publicity purposes than anything else.

He said, but I knew better. What I didn't know was they were there being paid for by Nancy for the sole purpose that Tom had intended for them to do for him

Where the wives that were there, more, or less stayed grouped up, and mostly to themselves. Knowing what was going on, and saying nothing to anyone about it. Not wanting to disrupt their life style.

Most of the time when it got down to the actual socializing. It was the women who were gathered up in groups, and the men were off talking business, or so their wives were lead to believe.

When I looked around practically all the men were gone, and only a few very young and very attractive women were still mingling about with the men who weren't gone.

As the other kept vanishing and resurfacing all going to gather up at the bar to eventually rejoin their wives.

Fortunes were made and lost during those social gathering, and I was naive enough to believe that going to them made me someone important to be admired.

I guess I deserve to be made fun of. Coming from a lower class family totally out of place, and naive as to how the upper class really lived.

CHAPTER 12

It wasn't until Tom's eventual death that I eventually met the one named Janet. I was playing tennis and I needed a partner, and she came from out of nowhere too my rescue.

I had no idea how she found out that I use to be Tom's wife, but after the match. She came right out, and bagged, and pleaded with me to help her get herself out from under a bad relationship she had with Tom.

She wanted out, but she couldn't. Not knowing what Tom did with what he had on her, and she had to find out if she was now obligated to me. Too continue what she was doing for Tom.

She told me everything what went on between her, and Tom. She even went as far as offering to pay me any amount, if I could find what he had on her, and would give it to her.

Where I had no idea if I could trust her enough to help her out. For all I knew she could be a plant for someone trying to get at the information for themselves, and I didn't want to be stupid enough to expose that I knew anything about what Tom had on her, or anyone else. Even though Janet sounded sincere about wanting to get her past life behind her.

She said she wanted to get married to her pervious boss's son, who she was working for at the investment booker firm she was working for that Tom got her the position she was now holding there.

Saying that her intent was only to set aside her ambition in life until she got enough money together where she knew she could live comfortably if her marriage didn't work out. That she didn't want her past suddenly coming up, and ruining her life.

I was still finding it unbelievable that I didn't know anything about what Tom was doing. Come to find out from Janet that Tom was having her laundering the money that he was receiving from blackmailing others. Through the booker firm she was placed into.

So that he could usher to funnel the money into the investment losses accounts. Having her written if off on the books of the investment firm. Then to have it withdrawn again in accounts lost, so that it never existed.

Where Janet would have it mailed to fictitious addresses. Where he would have it picked up, but by who she didn't know.

Saying that from there she had no idea where it went from there, but at the end of the week. Each time she sent an envelope entailing the list of accounts she founded the money into too Tom. Where every week on Friday he would come visit her either at her apartment, or at work too hand her an envelope. Containing cash that sometimes amounted to thousands of dollars for herself.

She said that she wasn't the only one. That Tom had others working for him doing the same thing, but now that he was dead she wanted out.

Saying that she knew Tom had a certain something on her that could put her in prison for a lot of years if it became known, beside what she became involved in since she's been working with him.

I knew from the accountants that came to visit me that Tom was stashing money all over under alias names. In safe deposit boxes, and factious accountant that were set up for him by Janet herself.

Who also had in her possession a ledger containing amounts distributed. That she was instructed to burn in the event that anything happened to him. Up to and including death, that she didn't burn as yet.

She said that Tom made it a point not to show up, until after any transactions were made. After one, or several of those who were working for him would come in, and come directly to me. To make their investment transaction into whatever accounts I was going to invest the money into.

Always keeping himself totally out of everything so that nobody really ever knew who was receiving the money on the other end.

As the monies were constantly being invested in other firms, into losing accounts. Where it would eventually just disappear as tax losses, and writing off in taxes.

What Tom didn't know for sure was if the person complied to his demand until a good two weeks later. That's how long it took to move the money through his system of things.

If after the two weeks, and the money wasn't there.

Without hesitation everything he had on the person he was dealing with. Would found its way to all the right people, and no one was the wiser about who it was that was doing the blackmailing. Which totally exonerated him of having anything to do with anything. Actually leaving a record trail of the person's illegal transactions attempting to embezzle, or launder founds. Getting that person involved in income tax fraud.

She said that it was an undetectable way of funneling money. While still holding the one paying responsible.

As the monies were delivered to different companies as payments. In the form of a check to the payroll department.

That was then convert into cash, and the money was put into the system. Where one of his lady contacts would apply it into accounts. Them would immediately transfer it into the system of account paid, and deposit as a check made out to cash.

Losing all traces of where, or how the founds were lost. With no one being held to blame, seeing how there was no telling how many people were involved in the initial transaction, or what account it could have been lost in.

Where only he would know from the receipts from all of us women would supply him at the end of the week.

Seeing how most of the accounts were connected to the company's stock transaction. Companies could loss a fortune one day, and make it all back, and more the next. All one had to do was to following the up's and down's of the stock market.

The person handling the transaction was contacted prior to the transaction by Tom himself when he would make his weekly visits.

Letting her know the money was coming, and where it was going to be deposited. To let her know when, and where to look for it to arrive. Where she did likewise when the money was sent out to an addressed that only Tom provided to her only.

Right there was the only flaw in Tom's plan, but it put the person who sent it out responsible if it wasn't delivered when it was supposed to be. She lost out on her end from the deal which was usually about 10% of the amount agreed upon.

Along with everything Tom had on her, was also sent out. Which put him totally in the clear. Even if she did involve him.

When she was the one who handled the transaction, and of curse know nothing about the illegal activities that she was involved in.

There would be no way she could prove a damn thing against Tom, and he would know who betrayed him.

* * * *

The way I was seeing what Janet was telling me, was that it was a perfectly devised plan that left Tom totally blameless of having any knowledge of any wrong doings. I had to hand it to him. Tom was a genius at the way he set things up.

Thousands of dollars were being funneled right under everyone noses. Without even the IRS catching on to what was going on. All appearing legal, and above board, and accounted for.

When as no sooner that Tom received the money he would reinvested it in some good stocks, as well as bad stocks. So that he could use what he lost on his own income tax.

Actually getting me to apply separately when making out our income tax. Claiming me as an independent investor that he himself place money in purposely. Keeping his tax returns separated from mine

To make even more money for himself. While making me believe that he wasn't as smart as he thought he was. Having me getting a simple return where he was getting thousand dollar returns behind my back

As for the women he was using to get something on someone. They didn't have any connection with him other than sexual. That's what he was using Nancy for.

Everyone was getting a peace of the actions, so no one was doing any complaining. Most of the women never even knew that they were being photographed by hidden cameras, or being over heard on tape recording.

They were instructed to take their client to a certain room, or place, and everything would be provided for them along with insurance that what transpired would be in private.

Tom thought of everything with the exception of me, and what I was doing without his knowledge.

I honestly believe that if it wasn't for me bringing him down. There would be no telling where he would be right now.

If I hadn't have unknowingly ended the greatest scheme of probably all times there would have been to limits to how far he could have achieved to rise too.

When I heard that work guardian angel. There was no mistaking the method Tom used to keep everyone in line.

Especially if anyone dared to betray him, or tried to get greedy, or wanted to get out because they were running scared, and the way he was having each other monitor each other he would have spotted any signs of betrayal right off.

That protective angle of his never left him. Like a demon form hell. It would most likely appear, then vanish after attacking a family member of those he had betraying him.

Making it impossible to hinder anyone from even thinking of leaving his private organization, or to double crossing him.

The way he had everything set up he would know immediately who it was, and all it took were a few examples to keep everyone in line without them not knowing who or why they were being preyed upon. Probably not once thinking that it could have been Tom who was making them rich, and opulently prosperously.

Even if they went to the police. The way he had it set up there would be no way anyone could implicate him, and then he had all that he needed to use against them.

As for the one who did. They would be the hardest hit, as well as their families, friends, and lovers.

Whereas the worse the cops could possibly do to his organization was maybe disrupt his operation somewhat if at all because there was really no known interaction going on almost any of those who was working with him.

Where he knew everything there was to know about them working them individually using whatever means he had too in order to keep them happy.

If one word got out. The entire operation would be shut down with the cops not being able to prove a damn thing. He had everyone actually responding to a simple code word. That's how the network was set up.

If just one phase of the operation got held up for any reason. The system would automatically shut down. Until whatever happened was found out, and the one responsible would be the one held accountable.

Come to find out that the entire conspiracy started when he found out that I was pregnant and lost the child.

That's when Nancy came into Tom's life and started faking his time cards. Then escalated from there until the day it all collapsed on the day Tom died, and the unbreakable chain snapped into a million paces.

Where I was the one who inherited the rewards of anyone labors by accumulating his Tom's vast fortune along with everything else.

His vast emperor consisted of an unlimited credit lines, and piles of private files on everyone he was in control of. Including vast amounts of holding in stocks, bonds, and other assets such as real-estate, and land entitlement.

Believe me if I would have known what I was doing was going to benefit any of those women he was involved with. I damn sure wouldn't have done it! I did what I did for me and no one else.

What I didn't know was that Tom also had what he referred to as safe house. Where he had a large safe installed in a secret compartments.

Tom was collecting money but, not spending very much of it. So that he wouldn't exceed his existing prudential of his present life style. That I could become aware of, or anyone else.

Even though we were living a very extravagant life style as it was. His holdings even included an apartment complex.

Not to mention how astonished I was. When I discovered that he had himself an actual yacht. That he bought in Sallies name. That was worth over a million dollars just sitting out anchored at one of the extravagant hotels at Shelter Island no less.

DISPLACEMENT INTENT

* * * *

Janet and I palled around for about a mouth. During which I was discovering more, and more of his endless list of crimes, and achievements. That wasn't getting any better but worse from not knowing how to handle all he was involved in.

Not knowing how to liquidate what he accumulated, or account for the crimes that he was committing while doing it that he had his so called financial managers heading for him encompassing criminal battery, extortion, soliciting prostitution, as well as possible for serval missing persons.

That he was implicated in but no charges were ever filed against him, but were against others who had either confessed and charged, or just up and quite their jobs, or just simply disappeared along with their wives and families but not by the authorities but, by the companies that were being investigated on criminal charges.

It was as if Tom set himself up his own private syndicate with everyone thinking that he was a drunk, a wife better and an adulterer. Who was using drugs, sex, and exploiting gambling to obtain control.

Establishing his own criminal emperor with everyone else looking for who might be behind, or responsible for the investigation going on against their companies.

I had to admire his genius, but it didn't alter my feelings towards him to become any less intolerable.

His deceit, and abuse of me, and his daughter wasn't the only thing that bought about my contempt. It was self-inflected! That damn cowards didn't have the balls to do what he forces me to do, and I wasn't about to kid myself where he was concerned.

That he knows all along what I was doing to him. There was no doubt about that in my mind... That's why he kept pushing, and pushing. Until it became the last straw that broke the camel's back.

I often thought about it being a lot easier to just up and have him killed, but there was no way Tom was ever going to let that happen.

Least ways not before he settled the sore first with anyone he might of thought could have been involved with me even thinking of doing something so stupid.

Maybe he just wanted to find out just how far I was willing to take my plan before he would put a stop to it, and got himself caught off guard with that bad fish I feed him.

I really had no idea what was going through his mind. We became so divided that if there was any concern between us. It was for Sally not either of us.

I was the one being subjected the most by his physical and emotional abuse. Not to mention the anguishing effect it was having on me to a point where I to was becoming emotionally stressed out.

Just as suddenly as Janet appeared. She no soon just stopped coming by to see me.

I called up her place of work, and asked for her.

Where it appears that she quit her job, and left without giving notice. It didn't take much to figure out that she got my package that I had mailed to her.

I honestly believe that the absolute turning point towards my resentment for Tom came about at a sociable party at Tom's bosses home.

When I saw him with my own eyes with a young girl. Who couldn't had been older than 15 at best.

* * * *

I was mingling as usual. Hobnobbing with the wives of the other executives, not paying much attention to what Tom was doing as usual.

No matter how I felt about what was going on I had to hand it to Tom for all he achieved. Going from a drill press operator and working his way up, and out into becoming an assistant accountant for a large investment firm company.

I had to admit it I was traveling in the glamor of his success. I always knew Tom was going to make me proud of him, but I never expected that he would achieve the impossible.

By giving me a world even snow white would be envious of.

Especially at such a time in my life that my whole life was being shattered about me. Where I was actually contemplating actually killing him, and actually in the process of doing it.

Never have I ever thought that Tom would stoop so low as to have any form of sexual contact with a girl so young. Especially not at the bosses own home.

It never once dawned on me. That at one time I was once as innocent naive teenage girl myself when he got to me the way he was getting to her.

The girl was his boss's niece. Visiting from New York for the summer. She was a very attractive young girl with over enlarged breasts for her features, being as short as she was.

Her bust as well as her behind were Tom's fetishes. Large breasts, and a firm butt on any women would capture Tom's full attention, and she got his full attention the second he laid his eyes on her.

Where once I thought about it I believed that it was her youthfulness that attracted him even more to her. She had that baby complexion appeal that had several older women them at the party talking about her.

Commenting on how they wish they still had that sexual appeal she was flaunting about walking around braless parading her big nipple breasts protruding out from that strapless dress she was wearing.

Tom wasn't himself anymore. Not anywhere like he was when I first met him, that was for sure.

It could had been that he was trying to recapture his youth, and go back in time, maybe hoping that she was still a virgin. Which I was certain that she was far from.

I Went upstairs to use the bathroom. When I heard someone moaning and groaning as I pasted by an ajar closed hall closet door. That was just down the hallway towards the bathroom.

It wasn't as if I wasn't familiar with the sounds I was hearing. I know very well what was generating that sound being expelled from those gasping expenditure sounds.

It was out of curiosity to see who the lucky women were that attacked my interested. Too peer into the open crack of the ajar door.

The overhead light was on. I startlingly spotted Tom squatting using his leg muscles to hold himself up as he braced his back against the wall facing in my direction crouched down in the far back corner

The young girl as straddling herself across his thighs siting on him. With her back to him facing the wall across from her. Vigorously giving herself to him, as he fondly squeezed her pompous breasts. Tantalizingly pinching their nipples whispering something into her ear.

I don't know what happened. I shockingly saw myself as a mother picturing my own daughter being victimized as he once victimized me.

I never became so enraged in all my life... Hearing about his cheating on me was nothing like actually seeing him doing it, and with such a young girl no less.

My blood boiled from enragement! I wanted to yank the door open and attack him, but something called fear! Forced me to panic and run towards and into the bathroom.

Frantically I paced not believing what I saw with my own eyes. Terribly afraid not knowing what to do?! Knowing what I wanted to do but afraid of myself and what might happen to me in the process.

Knowing Tom, and his temper, and that he would protected himself, and would most likely kill me in the process if I made him feel threatened by me.

Knowing what he was capable of doing, and what I feared most was him doing it to me. He's already hit me and there was no telling what he might resort to doing if I confronted him on what I saw with my own eyes. I was that fearful of him.

As I was stammering pacing back and forth. The young girl entered the bathroom. Startlingly I panicked and attempted to cover up my facial expression of contempt.

While holding myself back from wanting to claw her eyes out, and to cruelly tear her apart inch by inch.

As this whore of a girl stepped right in front of me and stood before the sink beside me uplifting her the hem of her dress, and proceeded to wipe herself off.

I couldn't help but to notice that she was obviously bleeding and was attempting to wash away the blood with a wet wash cloth looking at herself in the mirror holding the hem of her dress up under her chin.

"Are you alright young lady?" I concernedly ask. Knowing what just happened to her and that she just obviously lost her virginity.

"Nothing a few stitches wouldn't help but I'll heal."

"What happen...?"

"Well is that obvious...?" She cockily snapped back." It was bound to happen eventually anyway I was getting fed up being a damn virgin anyway..." She opened her purse saying taking out two large black pills popping them into her mouth."

"So who's the lucky fella?"

"Nobody you would know lady... Damn... but was he huge... though..., but at least now I'm going to be one size fits all thanks to him and not having to worry about everything being one sided all the time and being the one to be getting abused this time.

I came here for this to happen so that I can blame my Uncle because of it. Letting me get drunk and have sex with someone I never know.

So that my parents will let me live the life I want to live now that I'm not their precious little virgin.

What I really should have done was to make him pay for doing me the favor. I hope he realizes what he got out of me letting him get off scout free."

"Damn right you should have made him pay.!" I aggressively replied back. Hoping to encourage her to go after him to make him pay. Hoping to embarrass him in front of everyone who were there at the party as well as his boss

"I can see we aren't on the same sync level lady. Let's just say it was worth what I got out of it and leave it at that...

It's gone now there's no way of ever getting it back. Beside You'll never believed how that guy rocked my world...!

As soon as I stop burning I might even go back for seconds, maybe even thirds." She shoved a large glob of toilet paper up between her legs then pulled out her pants from her purse and attempted to step into them to put them on. Where she became staggeringly dizzy.

I caught her in my cradling arms as she swooned gasping..." Woo., What a buzz...?" She reached up grabbing the sides of her head dizzily saying.

That little slut was high on drugs. I didn't know what else to do so I dragged her over to the toilet, and aided her to sit down.

With her muttering sounds that I could only make out to be nothing but gibberish coming out from an incoherent voice before becoming solemnly passive, then nestled her head against the flat of my stomach still mumbling something.

The little slut was flying higher than a kite. She never stopped mumbling, she was so out of it so bad she nearly lost consciousness a few times.

I held her head to keep her from falling as she slid off the toilet onto the floor. Where I then rested her head on the seat, and left the bathroom.

Rejoined the festivities finding Tom standing with his boss drinking as I rejoined the party. I never saw the girl again after that night.

That was the one and only time I ever caught Tom in the act of cheating on me, and believe me once was enough.

As far as I was concern Tom was totally out of control, and he had to be stopped. Now he was into drugs, and molesting young teenage girls, and all it would take is one scream of "Rape" for him to send out that protective angle of his, or me comforting him about what I seen, and it would be all over for not only he both of us but, for Sally as well. I couldn't allow that to happen.

The only thing that stopped preventing me from doing just that was suddenly remembering where we came from, and how we got where we were at, and who was obviously still looking for us.

Thinking that I didn't mind Tom getting what he was deserving of but, I was a mother now, and I had to think of my daughter's welfare as well as my own knowing the unwritten law that I bond myself too when I became his wife which would go for my daughter as well.

I could see grown women who knew what they were getting themselves into, but young innocent girls were going way too far.

Knowing the worst that could happen to my daughter and I, and it wouldn't be a quick death but, a long torturous one being shared amongst those Tom and I betrayed having to submit ourselves physically until our usefulness were out being too drugged up to do anything to prevent it but, being aware what was happening to us.

Tom despised drugs of any sort and detested anyone who marketed them. What I couldn't understand was how he was able to avoid the authorities from becoming involved in all his illegal activities that he was subjecting his own family too suffer the same fate he was contributing too subjecting all those other helpless souls he was participating in selling drugs to.

I had to know everything Tom was getting himself involved in and I knew where to find out the answers to a lot I didn't know about.

After I went storming out of the party I took a cab directly home bond and determined to find out once and for all where my daughter and I really stood not only illegally but, otherwise where are previous life was concerned if anything happened to him.

Making a grin discovery that literally terrified me to the point where I had no choice but to hope and pray nothing did happen to him, because my daughters and my life depended on nothing happening to him.

Making it virtually impossible for me to go to the cops, or even thinking of running away from him and hoping that we could survive the onslaught that would be pursuing us.

With one possibly implicating me in all his illegal activities where I could spend the rest of my life in prison.

Where the other not spearing us the mercy of just killing us but, subjecting us to a lifetime of tormenting anguish distributing my daughter and I amongst the organization do drugged up we wouldn't even know our own minds.

Though there was so much Tom took with him that no one will ever know. I know before his death about his hidden rooms in, and about the house where Tom would go that contained secret compartment.

That he thought I didn't know anything about. That on the night I left the party that I searched for and discovered and never let on that I knew I was aware of but would secretly explore during the day when he wasn't at home and at night after I put Sally to bed for the night.

That after I found then and couldn't get into them that night. I waited until he left the next day and had duplicate keys made for the locks on the doors.

Discovering the first one but not the other two, until later on by closely watching where he would go when he would suddenly disappear for him to suddenly show up from out of nowhere sometime later.

During the years we had are home Tom had three, additional rooms added on to the already 3,600 square foot house that we already had.

A guest room, a cottage out by the pool, and a drawing room off the kitchen. Not counting enlarging the laundry room.

The guest house no one ever lived in it with the exception of Tom himself when we would have a heated argument. The plans showed significant alterations to the already 1,200 feet structure.

Tom wasn't one to leave anything lying around that would incriminate him in anything illegal and as far as I knew I had everything Tom had locked up in the family safe down in the basement that I knew the combination of that.

It was down in a cellar addition that I discovered the first of his stashes that he had complied that he felt were safely secure enough to leave out in the open just lying around easy accessible in filing cabinet, and on top of his desk even.

Where he even left the door to his secret room unlocked when he went off supposedly for some business conference.

Which I took off and down to the locksmith that I was having keys made for all the other locked doors he was keeping locked form me to get into. Where I took back and put back on by myself without him ever being the wiser.

Tom might have married me with I naive, gullible, and ignorant but, I had to get a lot smarter and fast over the years just to keep up with his scheming and conniving he was always doing always keeping himself ahead of the law as well as out of sight of the syndicate as well.

He was a sly as the devil and as slippery as a fox and as conning as an eagle of prey. One can't live with someone like that and not get smart fast.

Then all I had to do was went for him to leave and go find out what he was hiding form me. Little by little discovering what was in his secret files he had on everyone along with all that he was involved with.

DISPLACEMENT INTENT

Some of the files held very incriminating evidence against certain people. Hit and run accidents, embezzlements, drug dealing activities, illicit sexually encounters on both men, and women.

Police reports on everyone past lives, and/or hidden identities. Photos, and tapes of conversations implicating people in illegal activities.

All with names of a great many rich and the influential peoples, and how they went about circumventing the law, and how they were in the position to manipulate certain elections, and illegal transactions over acquiring land.

Tom had in his possession certain documents that still to this day remain a mystery as well as a constant threat to certain very influential people. That were associated between the churches, and some very large corporations. That stated.

That certain lands and holding were donated for tax reasons but, the church never obtained possession of anything.

That were declared as charitable donations along with the deeds of transfer, but were still being carried on the state books as taxable properties.

Proving that the rich used the millions that the poor and the tax payers donated to bail out dying corporations using tax loopholes to cover up the agreement.

Where those involved made millions on the transaction, and the transactions was untraceable. The document that Tom had in his possession held the key to who was involved. As well as how the founds were disbursed.

Too look at Tom, one would think he was just like the ordinary executive. He never appeared that he had any more than anyone else or never pushed his weight around.

He made a point to never stand out amongst his peers, but to those who knew Tom no one didn't want to divulge that they had anything to do with him.

Basically because they were fearful of offending him, or becoming involved with anything he was involved with.

Even though they couldn't prove any wrong doing on his part. Word got around that he was one to avoid if at all possible. Creating uncomfortable suspicion that became the morn within the brokerage industry, that I'm sure Tom was made aware of.

Tom could have become a prominent figure in and amongst state representative. If it wasn't for the stigma that preceded him, and where others fears, and apprehensions of his being a threat to them as well as to their future success.

Either in the same profession, or were harboring ambition to establish careers of their own there would had been no telling just how far he could have promoted himself

CHAPTER 13

Prior to Tom's death. Tom took Helen out too wined and dined her. Where they actually sat down, and talked like they use to do. Before they came out to California.

Afterwards taking her to an elegant restaurant where they drink champagne and even danced. Tom took her to a hotel where he had a suite reserved.

Where upon entering the suite there was another decorated table sitting in the middle of the room.

With champagne sitting in the middle of the table chilling in ice and only two glasses and two chairs across from each other.

Along with his valise sitting on top of a table where he sat where he sat before at the table across from her.

Opening champagne with me watching him pouring it wondering nervously what he was up to. As he handed me my glass and we sat across from each other sipping champagne facing each other.

As they sat staring at each other looking if not knowing what to say waiting for someone to break the ice, sipping champagne.

Tom reached out to pick up the valise, and placed it on the table in front of him opening it. Unknown to Helen it contained his forty-five, automatic. That was his old gun that she thought that he left behind when they left Milwaukee.

He places it on the table beside the valise. Then reached into the valise again pulling out a large orange folder and placed in on top of his valise as he closed it laying the folder on top of the closed valise, beside the gun.

* * * *

From here is what my mother wrote to me in the journal she left me after she died. She went on to tell me. How she sat wondering what was going on. While trying not to feel the lease bit nervous over what his intentions were.

Hoping that up this point all that transpired between the two, of them was romantically inspiring that was leading up to only one outcome between the two of them, and stopped there. Only to pick up again leaving what followed open to interpretation, and one has to ask themselves.

What really took place between them and why after all that's transpired that would bring them to this point?

She went on to write. That she felt certain that she was going to died that night. That as she sat looking into his eyes. She could see the horrors of his intentions, and wanted to jump up, and run in dire fear for her life.

As he just sat there calmly staring aimlessly, as if looking right through her. Placing his right hand on the gun laying on top of the that valise that was sitting before him on the table then said.

"I know Helen."

That's when I became really terrified as he picked up the gun and leaned back in his chair against the back of it, saying with a hollow daunting voice.

" I know it all..." As he sat pointing the barrel of the gun he was holding to his hand on towards the folder, saying.

"Go ahead read it I want you to."

As if threatening her to read what was in the folder lying beside his hand pointing the barrel of the gun. She picked up the folder nervously opening it.

It was full of medical charts which she couldn't understand. Plus, a detailed medical diagnosis report attacked to the back of the charts. Along with a doctor's recommendation for treatment.

She felt certain by the way he was looking at her. That she was the one who was going to suffer his fate. And for the first time in her life literally feared for her life.

"Helen if I was you I would have killed me a long time ago for all I've done, but you must believe me. I never meant for any of it to start, and when it did. I thought I could stop it from happening again.

For the life of me Helen I don't know how I could have wronged you the way

DISPLACEMENT INTENT

I did. I've known for some time that I wasn't deceiving you, but yet I continued to do so.

Knowingly knowing that it's gone too far, and it has cut too deep into our life and your heart for me to attempt to make excuses for what I did now. It's done and there's nothing I can do to change it back."

"What are you talking about?" I stressfully asked...

"Tom what are you accusing me of doing? I don't understand what you are trying to blame me for, and why are you showing me these medical reports...

Is there something happening to you that I should know about...?!" I frightful ask. Pointing to his hand on the gun.

"Why are you showing me that gun...?! Tell me Tom what's going on in that mind of yours...?

I've done nothing to you, nor do I know of you doing any wrong to be sorry for. I think you need a rest.... You haven't been looking or feeling to good lately... I need you to go see a doctor... Your doctor. What's was wrong with doctor Phillip's? Who's this doctor...?"

Tom leaned forwards reopening his valise to pull out a miniature tape recorder placing it on the lid of the valise closing it again, and turned it on. Letting her listen to what was on the tape.

"Phillip this is Helen. Tom just left the house. Contact me. I've no idea where he's going or how long he's going to be gone. I need to see you... It urgent that I see you..."

I had my own voice calling out Philips name speaking over the phone as I stood impatiently waiting for Phillip to answer his phone. Shockingly not believing that Tom actually bugged the phone.

"Thank god! you finally answered. Dammit I need an emergency appointment!

That no account husband of mine is becoming a real degenerate. He's got this affliction for young girl, he's become deranged, and I mean really young girls. I was willing to except him carrying on with other women, but he's becoming perverted.

I want this to end right now. I'm going to tell him about us and divorce him I just can't tolerate being near him any longer.

Nothing I'm doing seems to be working fast enough... I don't know how much more of this I can stand. He denying me and giving himself to all those other whores of his... Thank god, I have you or I would go stark raving mad. My god... I need you so badly...!

"Helen I'm only your doctor I'm not his conscious. What do you expect me to do to stop him?"

"I don't know but you've to do something...! or I'm going to tell him all about us, and don't give me that crap that your only my doctor shit!

You best come up with a way out for me and quick! And you can tell that doctor of his that I'm through catering too him! He's so damn bad at being his doctor he's keeping him alive.

Now I want my appointment, and the both of you to get your heads together and do something, or I promise you I'll make you both regret the day I came into your lives!"

"Calm down and stop worrying Helen." Phillip relied back." I'll make a couple of calls, and tell you how things worked out when I see you tomorrow around 2 PM, but not at my office. You know where, wait for me. I'll get there as soon as I can and be careful I don't want Tom finding out about us. Until then don't try to contact me."

"So you knew all along is that what you're trying to tell me? That you've been spying on me... So what tipped you off?"

"That's not important." Tom solemnly spoke up. Turning off the tape recorder." But yes I've known before I sent Nancy to the hospital to unknowingly inform you about her and the others. Knowing that Phil was also her personal doctor as well as the others.

I knew what you find out that day would affect you, but to what extent I was certain about. until I discovered what you were attempting to do along with the aid of my doctor. Until I felt certain that I couldn't trust him anymore a found myself another doctor.

At first I wasn't certain about you and Phil until he told me what was going on between the two, of you.

I could deal with you betraying me but when it went to the extreme of actually wanting to kill me. That's when I had to find out if you would go through with it. Even knowing I was responsible for you becoming so drastically obsessed with actually going through with it.

I'm also assuming that you have been discovering a lot that you're not letting on. That you knew about my activities that you wouldn't have by not snooping around behind my back.

Lucky for me that I trusted in no one but you, and you weren't the only one who's been betraying me from your lover Phil. To which he's been informing me ever since the first time you betrayed my love for you with him.

Eventually you left me no choice to find another doctor because my doctor was more loyal to you than he was to me and stood by you.

Though Nancy was keeping you informed by telling you what I tell her to tell you about what I've been up too.

I've been able to keep abreast of what's been going on in that devious mind of you.

Helen no matter what you were lead to believe I still do love you, and it's not too late for us to start over again."

"Tom I might not know it all, but I know enough. That's why I don't think that it would be possible for us to start over again. I've heard and seem too much, and you are wrong.

Far too much has been said, and done that could be undone. I could never trust you again. As for loving you I haven't for so long. I can't remember when it was I did.

In a way I'm glad that it's over. Now I don't have to lie to you or myself anymore. So I've failed in giving you what you deserve, but that still makes you a contemptible son-of-a-bitch! That I grow to hate, loath, and despise...!

Go ahead us that gun you'll only kill the body... You've already killed all I loved and treasured most of all in life years ago.

To the point where killing you was all I had left. I wanted to see you suffer like you made me suffer.

I can't begin to describe the anguish I suffered because of you... It was you who made me go to them while you sadistically ripped my love for you out of me...!"

It was you who created the desirous women you made out of me. You couldn't expect me to react any other way that I did. Just because you had yourself a hang-up about having sex when I was pregnant.

Everyone told you that it wasn't your fault and how ridiculous it was of you to blame yourself. If that wasn't bad enough.

You used that as an excuse for you to go around screwing all those whores' you been screwing continuously nonstop!"

"Helen we've too talk." He placed the gun down on top of his valise beside the recorder leaning back in the chair he was sitting in. Putting distant between himself and the gun.

I couldn't take my eyes off that gun. I know that Tom was actually giving me a chance to kill him, before he would kill her.

I lounged out her right hand grabbing up the gun. He didn't even try to stop me. I sat pointing it at him squeezing my finger back against the trigger. Holding the power of life, and death in my trampling hands.

With everything I seen, heard, and felt for him as far back too when I first heard Nancy talking to her girlfriends in the hospital.

Going through my mind, as flashes of seeing him with my own eyes of him ravaging that teenage girl, and still as badly as I wanted too. I still couldn't pull the trigger.

"You Bastard...!" I irately yelled at him. Inflamed with rage. Dropping the gun to the floor at my feet.

Emotionally breaking down covering my face with my hands. As I jerked up, and ran into the bathroom, slamming, and locking the door behind me.

Knowing when I would come out that I would never make it to the door to leave. That he was most likely just sitting waiting for me to end it once, and for all.

Sure enough there he was sitting in the chair staring at the bathroom door. With his gun in his hand. Resting it on top of his middle right thigh.

I nervously walked towards the table to pick up my purse and my fur cape, and skeptically walked towards the door.

DISPLACEMENT INTENT

With each agonizing step I took my heart came to a paranoiac stop. As if anticipating it was going to be my last step. As my ears strained to hear the thundering sound of him firing the bullet that would end my life.

Then as I placed her hand on the metal door knob, I panicky heard. A heart stopping metallic sound that came echoing besieging into my ears. Thinking it was coming from his gun.

Cause me too nearly die right where I stood from a heart attack. Only to hear in my besieged ears is echoing voice. Exploding in my ear drums saying.

"Helen please don't leave me..."

As the rapturing sound of his voice penetration did more than a bullet ever could. As I stood in a prettified state besieged with overwhelming anxiety over whether to turn the door knob any further, or not.

Panicky feeling certain that I didn't feel the impact of the bullet striking mem and I was going to die any second. Startlingly finding myself still alive asking myself uncertainly why...?!

"Helen twice you could have killed me. You can't leave without finishing what you started. Helen I don't want to die, but will willingly do so if my death would erase all that I did to you.

If killing me would give you the satisfaction that you so richly deserve, that only I can do for you in the way of making it all up to you. If that's what it will take. You can't leave without completing that which you're deserving off.

Kill me now Helen, or I promise you to that I'll haunt you until my dying day until I make you love me again, but don't leave me without making your decision. Doing so would only haunt you even worse than I ever could."

I turned to stare at him. Totally confused." Bewilderingly asking. "What are you trying to pull now?"

"Helen with me dead. We could start anew. You'll have all you so richly deserve, and everyone else will have peace of mind.

I don't want your pity, or your hated. All I'll settle for is your love, nothing less. Even knowing that I've betrayed you. You must believe that it will always be you who I love more than life itself. You loved me once knowing who and what I was."

"I don't understand what you're saying to me...?"

"Helen I've to die. It's the only way I can be stopped. I want out of this life, but I don't want to lose you. You killing me will erase all I've done, and might give us a chance to start over again. The only thing good I ever accomplish in my life is loving you, and Sally. Without either of you my reason for living doesn't exist anymore.

I know what I'm asking sounds ludicrous, and I'm not asking for your forgiveness. I know what I've been doing, and how it's been tormenting you but, if you walk out that door without putting yourself out of your misery. This moment will never stop haunting you.

With or without me you'll never be able to live with yourself. Only you can do what no one else was able to do. Take it, and go live in peace for a change." He held out the gun for me to take out of his hand.

"You'll be rich Helen, and free form me forever. As for what I'm asking I don't know what I'm asking. What I do know is if you don't come back to me, and walk out that door I won't be man enough to do it for myself.

This isn't my way of asking for another chance, but for you to accept the man you loved, and married. Knowing that I don't know how to live any other way.

I'm asking for you to open your loving heart to me, and let me love you in the only way I know how too.

By bestowing upon you. and Sally only that I've the means and ability to do. I do love you with all my heart I could never truly love another.

I know what I've done is reprehensible, and that I made your life hell. It's to hell I must will go, where I've live most of my life in it until you came into my life. You don't have any business going there because of me.

I'm all you claim me to be as. I'm a pathetic deplorable person who always tried to keep you out of what I am, but did so knowing that once you would see me for who I really am. You would come to hate and despise me like you do now.

I sit here contemplating my death not yours. Where it's you who I want to survive, and forget all about me, but this isn't the way to go about it.

Knowing you're not anything like me, but you will have to become because of me, and somehow I want to spear you that anguish that I alone must bear the blame for."

All the while Tom was talking instead of me walking out the door. I found myself being compelled to walk towards the table too sat down across from him.

Totally being drawn to him with curiosity.

Wondering what he was attempting to tell me. While pondering if I was right in what I was thinking, he was trying to tell her.

"Let me see if I understand you right. You want me to kill you, but not really kill you. Is that it?"

"Yes."

"Forget it…!" She snapped back at him.

"Then here…" He places the gun back in my hand, and held it pointed at his heart. Still holding his finger on the trigger. Where all I would have to do was to jerk his hand slightly for his finger to do the rest.

" Finish it right here, and now. Jerk my hand, and walk out. It will be classified with it being a suicide.

As much as I wanted to I just couldn't.

"Well while you're thinking about it I want you to listen to what I've to say." He released his hand for the gun saying.

"Helen we both know what you've been up too. I even know those who were conspiring with you, or should I say. You've been collaborating with at your expense.

I know you won't believe this but, I only did what I did because I wanted the best for you. I didn't mean for anyone else to become involved physically or otherwise.

First off we both know that I wasn't getting anywhere. The way you wanted me to do things. That life style just wasn't for me.

Sure it was a challenge, but when it started to become a drudgery, and boring I had nowhere else to go.

Because of you. I was allowing your way to take control over me, more than

I figured it would. Too a point where there was just no way I could deal with it any longer.

I wanted more than what I was just giving you. Up until our son died, and yes, I admit that things started to go wrong for us after that, due to me, and yes, the change that happen was mostly due to losing him.

I didn't care what you, or any doctor said. I was responsible for his death. I hated my job and myself. Not only for what I did to my son, but for making you live beneath you position. I wanted to go back to the way my life was, but I couldn't figure out how.

Then when Nancy approached me I saw the golden opportunity that inspired me to become enthusiastic again about my life.

I didn't mean to have sex with her, but I did. She kept wanting to express her appreciation for the opportunity I was offering to her.

First with a kiss. then with a little bit more enthusiasm. Making it harder not to take advantage of her affection, and it kept progressing until we finally came together physically but, not emotionally.

For me at least, and you were still healing physically, and I was still deeply emotionally depressing over the loss of my son.

I know it's not an excuse for allowing myself to succumb to her advances and I'm not attempting to use it as one. I'm just telling you how it all came about.

As it all turn out. It was working out great for the both of us. She was racking in the bucks. While I was having the thrill of being back into my old way of doing things again.

It was though her that I saw the chance to promote myself, and took it by doing what I know how to do best.

As I became more involved with advancing myself. Eventually everything else just became involved. It wasn't just all about having sex.

Sure there was quite a lot while building the organization, but once everything settles down it wasn't all that frequent, with me at least.

While I didn't hesitate to use them, along with their friends to grow the business we were developing

Helen I was only using them to bring us to where we're now. Using the only means I could use. I don't regret anything I done other than cheating on you.

Then trying to get you to leave me. Because I felt guilty about what I was doing with those other women. By setting it up for you to overhear what Nancy was saying to those other women.

Feeling certain that once you found out that she was also seeing Phil on the side, and possibly she could discover that she could find out about you through him, and that you were cheating on me behind my back. Would prompt you to leave me.

Where I could still be close to you, and be able to make sure you were safe and taken care of. Until I could figure out a way to get myself out from under without getting caught,

Helen having you leave me was the only way I could handle you not hating me for not loving you. Where at the same time I was hoping that you would come to love me all over again, and finally dump Phil.

You did it when we first met, and you had no idea what was going on in my life when I wasn't with you.

Even when you met Carol and found out that she was using her place for prostitutes knowing that I was working for her, and the syndicate as well.

Honey you don't understand. No one ever gets out. We left but, we never got out. Once they found out where I was. It was either do what they wanted, or pay but, if any word got out it was going to be all over for us both.

So I've been paying to those who found me. That's how everything really got distorted way out of proportion.

Honey I wanted to come back into your loving arms, but everything became so damn involved, and my main concern was protecting you and Sally over everything else. It's all so quicken meaningless without you two shear it with.

I had no choice, but to figure out ways, and means to manipulate around everyone. Once the syndicate became involved.

I did all I could for them not too. I even went as far as eliminating a few, so that they wouldn't get word back to Wisconsin.

Doing so only gave me a little time to protect you. That's when I made it possible for you to hear what you did.

As it worked out you didn't leave, and they caught up with me, and I was forced into making a deal instead of having anyone else get themselves hurt or killed, and I wasn't about to go back to belong betrayed like that last time.

It all started totally by accident. I went out to lunch with one of the head associates taking Nancy with me. When I came face to face with one my step father's close associates, and he told me the reason behind the attempt on my life.

There was a move against my step father because he couldn't be trusted anymore, and I was in their way. Seeing how I was his personal body guard. They never did know about anything else that went on between the two of us, and still don't. Otherwise I would have never ever made it home to you that day.

Shortly after we left my step farther along with all those who stayed loyal to him were killed with the exception of Carol, and us.

It wasn't until word got back that someone recognized me that they sent someone to verify where I was. Even though I thought I got to them before they sent word back.

Honey it's for that very reason I'm even suggesting what I'm going to suggest. I'm doing so in hopes that you still love me, or there's still a spark flickering somewhere in your heart for me.

Helen with me dead you'll have it all. Everything will be over and done with and I'll be a nobody, and a has been but, a filthy rich one.

We could share it all without anyone being the wiser. I've it all worked out. All I need is you saying that you'll go along with me."

"Just suppose I agree what will stop you from starting all this bullshit over again."

"You, and your love for me. Honey we had nothing when we came here. Now we've millions, and still more once it's all over. We can go somewhere else and start a new life for ourselves with Sally.

I grant you in might take some time, but it can be done with no one being the wiser, and with me out of the way. Anyone who could have known what was going on would have nothing else to fear from me. I'll see to that...."

Tom stopped before finishing what he was going to say. Having second thoughts about saying anything that would discourage me form saying yes, to his idea. Speaking out cautiously saying.

"You just let me handle that end. The least you know the better off you'll be.

I made one mistake, and that mistake nearly cost me the only one I ever loved. I left a trail for someone to follow.

You know that the people I grew up with have eyes and ear everywhere, and if they didn't trust me. We would have both been dead long before now.

They were lead to believe that my step father entrusted in me detail information against the syndicate, and I still haven't convinced them that I don't know what it is they're thinking I have on anyone.

I couldn't work for them, so I had no choice but, to give the monies that I had anyway to those who were blackmailing me.

Threatening to inform the heads of the syndicate where I was so I paid until I could use the only method I know how to. To stall for time before other start showing up.

By blackmail those women I got to them so I could get them to do what I wanted them to do.

I have no idea. I can only guess that a great deal of the money went back to those who were settling for me taking off. So I could avoid having to go back

Then they wanted in on what I was doing, but I told them that it wasn't all that great of an operation as yet, and it was only netting me barely enough to pay those I've working for me, and now them a percentage of.

Giving them the impression that it wasn't even paying off for me, so that they wouldn't be asking for more.

Then I had to pay the women, and they didn't come cheap believe me. Then I had to pay for different identities that were essential to distribute the monies in different places

It was costing me a fortune, and I couldn't let you catch on to what I was up to. You were the happiest I ever seen you in a long time.

I did what I had to do to move myself up in the company I was working for.

Using the pretext that I was working late. Making life difficult for people that were in my way to get ahead until they finally realized I was serious. The hard way.

Once I got Nancy in the right position the others were easy to get to work with me. I needed to make sure that you, and our daughter would be provided for if anything happened to me while at the same time giving you a life that you so richly deserved.

I was managing stashing away chucks of money at a time. Things were going to well as I was pulling in more money blackmailing high racking officials in other companies, as well as city officials, and I started making some good investment.

I needed ways in, and never let anyone out. I felt sure that I had everything under control. Until I discovered that things became far more involved than I figured they were, and there was no way I could back out even I wanted too.

It was mostly the money, and it was piling up so fast. I wasn't finding enough places to stash or invest it. I had to do something with it, knowing if I didn't I would surely be found out.

That's when I started to slowly let a lot of them off the hook, but never let them forget that I haven't forgotten about them.

My bosses father was the one who opened the door. He was a big time investor in junk bonds who knew people in high places in the investment firms.

That's how I moved out of being a supervisor into the investment business. Once inside I used Nancy to connect me up with private secretaries.

In other investment firms who were in the position of authority over accounting managers, and manipulated them into manipulating those in the position of funneling large sums of money.

All along I was paying Nancy 10% and the others from 3 to 5 % netting myself 30% which was multiplying quickly.

What I didn't know was. That son-of-a-bitch pf a boss was into buying and selling drugs, and into prostitution as well.

The city was loaded with ripe illegal Mexican girl, as young as ten years old. Those girls jumped at the chance of making money. My bosses' son always had a couple around for his own personal pleasure.

DISPLACEMENT INTENT

His son was running the operation. He was the one who sent his 15-year-old niece after me. I admit I got high on sorting coke with him, and his niece.

It wasn't until some of his cohorts came in and interrupted us that he asked her and I to leave, and that's how she latched onto me in that closest.

I was so stoned. I never resisted when she lured me into one of those linen closets upstairs at his father's home. On one of the nights we were there with me and obviously saw the two of us together.

It only happened once. I want you to believe me about that. I can't say the same about the others, but with her I made sure she never got close to me again.

Honey you've to believe me when I say that I knew what was happening, but she meant nothing to me, nor have I ever used drugs again.

I was really out of it, and I didn't like not being in control of what's going on around me. I still don't know her name.

It wasn't until later that it was her eleven, year old sister who was my bosses' son mistress. That I caught him with her one night, and got pictures of him going at it with her. That if his wife ever found out. She would be owning the company his father built.

He thought to use me to get at the one who was blackmailing him. By getting something on me with some young girl, and he would have. If I wouldn't have spotted the light of a camera flickering. That slut knew what she was doing when she leads me into the closet.

That asshole was using my own method against me that I was using to set all those I set up to blackmail to blackmail me.

Hoping to take a movie of the whole thing, but while she went to freshen up I found the camera and removed the film.

The bastard had to have laced that cigar he gave me with coke, and by the time she leads me off I had no idea what was going to happen.

Helen I'm not going to lie to you, or am I going to make excuses for myself. It happens and I hold myself entirely too blame for allowing it to happen, but you know how things were between us sexually. Then there was Phil and you.

When I learnt about you carrying on an affair with Phil right under my nose. Then continuing to do so while conspiring to actually murder me.

All sort of outlandish thoughts went through my mind. You had me even doubting if the child you were losing were even mine.

As much as I wanted to stop it I couldn't because I had to find out for sure, and by the time you finally had Sally things were disastrous between us.

I knew why you wanted to keep Phillip on as your personal doctor. I even know you had him tie off your tubes.

Even when you were claiming all those miscarriages. Was because you didn't want to have anything to do with me. Because you came to hate and despises me so.

Even though with the understanding that denying myself was doing to me had to be doing even worse on you, but you didn't care about yourself but only wanting to make me suffer for what I did to you. Even knowing that you were doing the exact same thing to me.

After Sally was born I thought that I could regain what we lost by applying all my efforts on concentrating all my attention on you, but it didn't work out that way.

Things got rather complicated after that young girl I was with died of an overdose of heroin, and things went sort of out of control around the company. To the point where the cops became involved in investigating her friends, and associates.

Certain people also wound up disappearing, and still haven't been found because they too were involved with her, and no, I wasn't involved in any of them, so don't ever start thinking it.

By the time things died down long enough. To where I could have concentrated on you again. Are marriage being all but over, and them when I found out what you were up too I totally lost it.

It wasn't bad enough that I already killed my unborn son. Now I was force to having to deal with you doing likewise to me.

There was no way I could ever due you any great harm. I couldn't live with myself, and believe me. It did get to me.

Even as hypocritical as it sounds with me attempting to get you to hate, and loath me enough to leave me. It did.

I started to drink more, and I was becoming a nervous-wreck, and got agitated about everything. That's why we were always arguing.

Them when the hitting started, and I slapped you. I just totally gave up. I knew that what I did hurt you more deeply than the slap.

From there on things just kept on happenings. If it wasn't one thing it was another... All I needed was sometime to myself, but was I getting it.

Honey you need to understand what I'm trying to tell you. I was being used just like I was using them. They were using me, and I'm not going to any prison.

With me dead I could never appear again I'll be out of it, and they'll be on their own. Even if they did get caught. Which they will. I'll still be a free man."

"That's alright for you but what about me?"

"With me gone. What could anyone possible gain by coming after you. Especially if you decide to leave, and go back home to live happily ever after. While I'll be close by, but setting up things elsewhere like overseas.

You'll have million to support you and Sally on. While I disperse the rest of the money in other avenues overseas for when we all go to live after a few years. After I get us set up.

We can live like royalty for the rest of our lives, and if things start getting to hard for you to handle. We'll figure out a way to kill you off too.

Honey believe me there's no other way. You stand to lose possibly everything we worked so hard for, and it would have been all for nothing. They will converge on you like vultures tearing you apart until you give them what they want.

With me dead, and with you not having knowledge about anything that I was up to. They'll leave you alone.

Even with them thinking that you were the one who killed me, but it can't be proven. They wouldn't fuck with you out of fear that something just might pop up that they don't want popping up that will totally ruin their lives.

With me being still alive to assure that something does. All it will take is just one to try, and fail to scare the others off.

That also includes the syndicate as well. With them thinking that you are known to be in the possession of having certain incriminating knowledge that could be used against them, but not knowing against who.

As long as you promise to leave them be and that it wouldn't be in their interest to attempt to hurt you of force you to tell them anything.

Saying that what you know would be sent out to interested parties if anything might happen to you.

That you will see to it that upon your demise that what documents you might have will be sent to the person or persons it is direct towards. They will leave you alone.

All you'll need to do is live within your means until you sell the place, and get my inheritance. In order for you to leave to go live back home to your mother and brothers

With me dead you will still have the means to keep them off you, and with you not having any connection to me, or them.

They will know but, not for certain. That you could be in possession of documents to insure that they will leave you alone.

Where I'll be around to make sure that something might show up if they don't if they want to keep secret in their life from popping up. I've enough on all of them to put them all in prison for 3 lifetimes.

As for me. Once everything settles down who knows what money can buy? I'm getting kind of tiered of the way I look now. I could use a change.

You could take Sally back home with you, and tell her a convincing story about me. When you feel she's ready to be able to handle it, and get her to except the way things were, and if I should happen along.

A different person than when we parted, and we should fall in love again. Who knows you might even decide to want to marry again.

We could go live overseas and have her going to all the best school, and bring her up in the elegance she deserves where money would never be an issue again.

With me having a new look. I know I can get her to accept me as her step father, and just pray tell those from my past don't leave you alone. We could do the same for you.

I might have to change my appearance a couple of time, but the way I see it.

DISPLACEMENT INTENT

If you're ever to get ourselves another chance, and keep what is rightfully ours. It's the only way to totally have me disappear forever.

Even you could become a totally new person who I know Sally will accept you as her step mother.

Things will work out I promise you. With you acting as the bereaved widow, and me covering your back in the background.

Within a couple of years everyone will forget all about us, and all those millions I took with me will be for us to live happily ever after.

Honey we deserve a new way of life for ourselves. We earned it, and now is our chance to take advantage of it.

If we just go on with the way things are now, and I die where you live on. It's a perfect solution. With only a few minor problems for me to work out."

"What about your body?"

"No problem I've the prefect doctor who will handle everything. He'll sign the death certificate no questions ask, and you'll want a half close casket. With just my facing showing at the service before you cremate me.

After all you're going to have your daughter's welfare to think about, and have me burned disposed of as quickly as possible.

All you are going to have to do is keep her resentment towards me active. Maybe increasing it more would help her be content with the cremation part.

As for anyone else. All everyone is going to really care about is the fact that I'm dead. Just apply a lot of makeup, and keep the casket half close, and with a good strong sedative, I'll sleep through the entire service. Where I'll get out before they burn the casket, and the rest will be history right along with me. My death by a heart attack will be sanctioned, and we'll be multi-millionaire

After the funeral I'll disappear. Where you'll be able to find me a couple of days later where I'll be easy to find.

I'll be holding up in the pool house. While you'll be spending your time somewhere else too grieve stricken to want to go back living in the main house.

You'll have to get rid of the servants. Just tell them you'll be closing the main house down until you return. Which might be a couple mouths. While handing them their severance pay checks.

Of course you'll have to stop seeing your doctor Phillip beforehand. Other than that you just let me handle all the other details.

Once I'm dead it's only going to be a matter of time before the organization I created will fall apart.

They'll be turning against each other trying to drag the other down to take control themselves. And you won't have to worry about them turning on you. Not with me covering your back. As far as you know you don't know anything about what I was involved in while I was alive.

The decision is yours. I can't force you to want to try again but, either way you decide I'll be alive to protect you against them.

This way you won't even become involved in anything that might take place. Alive there's no way I'm going to allow anyone to prove anything against me, they aren't your concern where they will be mine.

Of course you'll have to pay the capital gains taxes from the sale of the house. All the rest of the money has no taxes attached to any of it.

It's all tax free money that you'll be receiving under fictitious names from different checking accounts, and secured bonds from overseas investment in our daughter's name. Well there is the life insurance policy, you might have to pay something out on that.

Honey if anything happens to me. I want you to know that I've a secret room under the Pool house. I also have given my attorney an envelope that will contain the combination of a safes in that secret rooms.

That I'm sure you are already aware of and what's inside them. I didn't what you to know until now. That I found the keys you had made, and the locksmith that made them, and I'm going to leave it at that.

If you decide to go along with my plan I'll empty everything I have out, and move it all to a new location. That will also be inside that envelope for you.

To do what you seem fit until while met again. Don't hesitate to use what's there against anyone who you feel threatened by.

Helen I do love Sally with all my heart but, until she forgets about me we can't risk letting her see me after I'm dead.

You will need to remove everything associated with me over a couple of years. Doing it gradually will help her to forget more quickly.

While you're settling your affairs I'll be going through several changes. Where upon after you leave. It will take me a while before I'll be able to show up after you get home back to your family

Where I'll not be the same person you left. There we'll have to keep meeting each other a secretly."

"What will you do to support yourself?"

"That's no problem I've enough money to live comfortable on for a long while, as for you. You'll still be getting my yearly income from the company, and all the monies you already have in different safes around the house, and wait too settle up with the insurance company before selling the house.

What I'm going to depending on you on most of all is too make sure there's not a lot of publicity about my death. Keep in quite as much as possible. I'll still have to move around until everything get settled.

Don't worry I'll never be very far away from either you, or Sally. If there's one thing I know how to do, that is to blend in. I'm not about to let anything happen to either of you."

"I don't know Tom...? It's been so long, and there's just so much I can't forget, and then there's me. I've been trying to kill you, and would have if you wouldn't have caught onto what I was doing."

"Trying yes, but killing me no. Honey I don't think you could have gone through with it.

At least now you know that what you got was only half truths.

You heard what they wanted you to hear, and you wanted to hear, but now that you know the truth, and who's been lying to you about me. You'll at least know where your enemies are coming from.

You know what was going on, but not why, and you knew that I wanted you to leave me, and you kept taking my abuse, and me back. Not because you had ulterior motives.

It was because we couldn't be separated since that first day we met. We've been bonded together.

Honey are affection for each other goes deeper than love. You could have killed me anytime you wanted. You're the only person who could.

You were a women betrayed by a man to who you gave all you could give. Who turned on you. You were ferrous. You felt as any women would have felt, but you're not just any women.

You can't love and hate at the same time. So you sought to avenge, but you were always there for me when I needed you. Never denying me anything, even though you resented doing so,

While all the time. You wanted me to suffer.

A woman such as you are don't destroy the one's they love. They attack and kill. They don't spend years watching them die.

You love me and always will. You're just letting your resentment and discontent deceive you into believing you don't.

Your one cruel, sadistic lady my dear. One I might add, if you didn't love me. You would have derived the utmost pleasure in skinning me alive inch by inch but, you heard only what you wanted to hear, and believe, and couldn't believe what you saw.

When it was me wanting to go back to the way my life was, and a onetime moment of indecision that brought us here talking like this now. I drove you into your contempt by my abstinence, and guilt."

"Tom what did you say or do to Phillip?"

"I didn't do anything but, talk to him. I wasn't even near him when he was attacked by someone with a meat hook.

The man came very close to not being a man anymore, or so I heard. I swear honey it wasn't me... The way I heard it. It was some women who he was going to marry who got to him. I was sure that he would have told you about it."

"Yeah, right I just bet that you didn't have anything to do with him shying away from me."

"Honey you've to admit. What worse punishment could he received than to suffer by the one he pledged himself too.

Now her I did met, and I must agree she is a lot like you. If you like I'll introduce you to her."

"Maybe later as for my answer. I'm not going to give you my answer until I hear everything and I mean everything.

I want the truth and nothing but, and if I catch you in one little lie. I promise you I'll never see you again for as long as you live.

I want to hear everything from the time it fists stated. Even though I heard most of it already."

"Honey you are talking a lot of years."

"Yes I know that's, and need I remind you. Those are years you took from me, and I wanted them, and I don't want you leaving out anything. Not even what you know about me. Now start talking..." I took the gun from his hand and placed it back on top of his valise.

The two of us spent two, days in that hotel room after which. They went home, and she continued her vendetta.

CHAPTER 14

I was still a young, and a very attractive woman. Who might even consider maybe even marrying if I ever became seriously involved with a likely male prospects.

Having no longer any reason to want to live in California, and wanting to get away from all the bad memories, and those I know resented, and despised me.

While unknown to all those he was involved with. I burned everything that I could find that Tom accumulated against everyone. After selling everything I took a trip to Switzerland.

Then moved back home to Milwaukee with my daughter not letting anyone know how well off Tom left me, or where I was going.

Just leaving without saying so much as a good-bye. The same way I left my life, and family when coming out to California with Tom.

Upon arriving back in Milwaukee I bought a moderately stylish home in a somewhat exclusive area where Sally could grow up properly. Living in a good home, and being able to send her to a reputable school.

Where later on she could hopefully go to any collage of her choice after graduating from high school. Before I took my daughter to meet my family.

Preparing Sally and I for the worst. If my mother would turn us away because of the way I just upped, and left her, and not even attempting to contact her over the years I abandoned her, and my brothers.

My mother adopted Sally. The instant I presented her. Standing with her on the front stoop of my mother's front door step, holding Sallies hand.

Nervously apprehensive over what was going to happen. When my mother opened the door and saw me standing on her door step holding my daughters hand in toll.

Making sure that we were both dressed moderately affluent, and having a brand new convertible sitting parked out in front of her house. Too give my mother the impression that I was doing alright for herself.

The second my mother opened the door, and saw me standing before it. She nearly had herself a heart attack. Startlingly screaming out. "My God...! Helen...?!"

Which brought my brothers charging towards her struggling to hold herself up using the front door. Catching her just in time before she collapsed.

While I just stood there not saying a word. Staring dumbfounding at the family I left behind. All grown up, not believing how much my brothers have grown.

After my mother got her second wind. She didn't waste any time rushing up to me. Hugging me to herself. Squeeze the life out of me, as she emotionally busted out in overwhelming tears of joy.

While my brother just stood there not really recognizing me at first. Then shockingly blurted out. "My God... It's Helen...!?" Ecstatically joining ma, joyously greeting me.

Hugging each other in a pile. Dragging my daughter and myself inside the house. Excitingly bombarding us with repetitious questions. Wanting to know everything about what transpired while I was gone.

For hours we all sat around answering, and asking questions amongst each other. While I became reacquainted with my brothers my mother talked to Sally.

It was from that second on that the two of them became inseparable. Where my mother started to pay more attention to Sally than she did me. Before turning the topic of the conversation on Tom, and asking me where he was.

That's when I told her about Tom dying unexpectedly, and tried to leave it at that. Hoping that my mother wouldn't pressure me too much, to want to know more.

Which at the time she didn't? Because of all the excitement and the rest of the family being around to overhear the details of Tom's death sensing that I would emotionally upset me and decided to waited until everything settled down, and the others settled down for the night. For us to have a private talk just amongst ourselves.

* * * *

Where Helen later told me that she told her mother that Tom died in his sleep from unknown causes. That was believed to have been the cause behind him having a massive heart attack.

She told me to stick to that story. Saying that no one needed to know the troubles we were having before my father's death.

Saying that his memory was best left with her mother thinking about him the way he was when she last seems him.

She said that she asks her mother not to voice her opinion about the way she felt towards Tom to me. Once again saying that the past was left best forgotten, and she didn't want me to think wrongly of my father.

Where I was still too young to have to deal with such emotional matters. That it was best that I let her handle things concerning my father, and our life together.

* * * *

Sally and I stayed with my family for about a week, on a night to night bases before I agreed to permanently move in with them.

Where we remained until I decided to ask my mother, and brothers to move into the house that I already bought.

Saying that she could rent out her place and come with Sally and I, and that she could even quit her job if she wanted too. Insuring her that I had enough money to take care of everyone.

During the years that followed my mother continued to work, and taking care of her sons while they pursued careers of their own. As I went into business for myself.

Opening myself a small antique shop while living a moderately quite life. Never marrying again, but having a comfortable social life.

Hobnobbing with the neighbors, and acquaintances I met when attending social gatherings. Meeting friends of my mothers and brothers, and other women from Sallies school.

I even became involved in a few short time associations with a couple interested gentlemen but, things just didn't work out because of one, reason or another.

One reason being that I was back living with my madam name of Jones. So that I could blend back into my mother's life style not having to answer a lot of personal questions associated with my life I spent with my husband.

Where Sally and I were eventually accepted as a widow with a daughter who came back home to live with my mother and family Where I could somewhat live happily ever after. Until I became stricken with cancer.

After thinking that they caught the cancer in time. I hoped to find new interests in I life, but a little over a year later.

The cancer came back, and I had to go through the treatments all over again but, the remission didn't last and it spread throughout my entire body.

It was August 1981 Three months after my mother Helen died at the age of 39 from cancer.

After which Donna my mothers, mother, and her three sons already adopted Sally while continuing to live with Sally in her mother's home. That Donna officially adopted Sally and continued to rise her as her own until she went off to college.

* * * *

At this point my mother's role reverts to me to take over for her. This is where the turning point in her life has to be open to interpretation.

Where I heard that my daughter is going to attempt to continue telling her story in her own words hopefully to correct any wrongs that she might have been accused of relating to the outcome where my father death was concern.

Where only I can do that seeing how you still haven't heard all that transpired where I read my mother's total journal after her passing.

Beside myself no one else knew what she related to me about what transpired before my father's passing That really might bring some light to what really took place between my parents. Even after all these years after her passing. Which could bring everything into prospective if in fact she did follow through with what her intent was in hopes to find some sort of retribution for all that he put her through.

For reasons intended to confused for the stories sake for the propose behind what her reasoning might have been as well as my own. I've decided to write her version of her story.

Even though there might been extenuating circumstances that might not collaborate with what might being said previously.

For the reason that should become obvious to some, and not to others. Even after all this time as lapsed someone might feel some connection. I want to assure you there isn't any.

I wrote her story not to be self-explanatory so that some might become confused for it was my intent to do so by making the names, places, and associates fictitious.

Whereas if you read what I written from my mother's journal. All that transpired up to, and too the completion of this their story.

I seriously doubt if it will come to enlightening anyone as to the validity of the content described within.

Too be totally honest I personally can't commit but, to certain portions that I personally took place, as for the rest. That I'll leave up to you the readers interpretations. Hoping that you will keep one thing in mind.

The fact that my mother was never held accountable for my father's death. As for the legacy my father left her. Like she already stated.

The actual amount was never known, not even onto me. She safe graded that information through multiple attorneys both feign, and domestic. Who founded my allotment over the years and still continue to do so? Whereas the reader can assume. (Whatever).

It wasn't until I was sixteen, five years, after my mother's passing that I was approached by an attorney, who claimed represent her estate.

Where it was stipulated in her will that I was to be handed a letter before I was to be able to receive an additional journal.

That was place in trust along with my inheritance. That was only to be handed over to me upon me asking for it, or I was found mature, as well as prepared to received it from the trustees administers my mother's wishes. Which was the firm representing her estate. Before the third reading of her will.

In that initial letter she told me a lot about my father. That really enlightened me to the sort of person my father was. Of which a great deal really shocked me, where the rest didn't. Remembering him from the way he was prior to his dying. Because the side I saw of my father was not one I honestly didn't want to remember him by.

Where I also found myself feeling sorry for him when he died but, only up to a point. Where not only conjectures, and second thoughts took over regarding his death. Where the constant fighting was going on between him, and my mother.

Where at times I found myself wishing that he would just leave, and never come back, when I was only eight, years old at the time

Where she stated the reason for the letter was only to prepare me for what I would read in the forthcoming journal. Following this letter.

That would go into more detail when I would be able to fully understand the purpose she wrote the journal. That was to be intended for my eyes only.

Pleading with me to please understand why it was she never did really fall out of love with my father. Even though it must have appeared that she did by the way they were treating each other.

The letter started out saying.

* * * *

"My daring Sally the reason I'm going to such length at this point in telling you about how my life was with your father. Is for wanting you to know everything that transpired between your father and I.

Along with the sort of man your father really was. I don't want you to have any misconception where he was concern He truly was a man to be admired as well as to be feared.

I'm purposely leaving out a lot about his previous past life, and only addressing parts that would help you understand what sort of man you father was underneath the persona he was showing of himself.

I can't express enough how I've always wanted to keep you from knowing what I'm about to tell you but, it's something you need to know. If I don't want you to hate me for what I it was believed but, never proved that I did.

To begin with when I first met your father. I was a naive girl just going on 18 years old. Who previously lived a sheltered life that I hated. Having to take care for my three, younger brothers.

Never in my life have I ever contemplated that I would become involved with a man such as your father.

To give you a brief insight about the man I venture into, then fell in love with. Was a miraculous experience from the very first!

All that you have previously seen, and overheard during those heated arguments the two of us had, that you should have never heard or became a part of. All I can say is that I'm sorry. However as hard as it was to believed what I said, was not exaggerated upon.

In his previous life yes, and even after we came together. He was nothing less that stupendously spectacular to be with when we were together, but while apart he was unscrupulously reprehensible.

Even with the unexpected revelations that literally struck utter terror in my heart and mind that he was being referred to mainly by the way they mentioned it.

The first was the name his associates and co-workers referred to him was the reason because he had no friends, and it wasn't his real name.

It was a name that was infamous with his criminal activity with those he associated with. To which he was kept on being referred to by a lot of those who associated with him when I was out with him.

Along with the synonymous name that he himself referred to several times, when he would tell me certain events that transpired while growing up.

One was the name he referred to as his protector was the "Guardian Angel" who brutally sought revenge on those who would dare to do Tom any bodily harm by unscrupulous striking out at them from out of nowhere, unmercifully brutalizing them.

Where the name those who knew him referred to him was the "Phantom." Which in with those he associated with was synonymous to an enforcer, or a hit man

Though those names might not mean anything to you right now. The more I enlighten you the more you will understand the man your father really was.

In order to understand what your father was like, and how he became the way he was. You have to have some insight into the way he thought of himself, and why it could have only been me to do what could be done.

Too but it bluntly. Your father was dead when he was born. He just wouldn't die, and when he was faced with it. He went into it not refusing to die, but embracing it.

He never known what it was to feel being loved, or how to express it. Who grew up to be a man without a conscious. Never harboring any remorse over the outcome from anything he's done.

Where it was I who gave him life, and it was only fitting that I was the one to take it away. Seeing how it was him who took my heart, and soul with him. That he used to give him life, and unmercifully denounced me for loving him.

I want you to fully understand why I did what I did. Not for the purpose of not judging either your father, or I. I'm sure once you read the journal that will be forthcoming to you. Will help you understand it had to be.

No matter how it will turn out for us. I thought you should know the truth once, and for all. So please humor me.

Them afterwards you can judge me for denying you all the years that past, and will past without us being there for you.

If the truth was to be ever told about the man your father was. It would be as incredibly unbelievable as the man himself, as well as what you will be reading about him.

When I said, that he should have never been born, and was supposed to have died at birth, but didn't, but to no fault of his own was forced endure surviving three, honorable attempts at taking his life before he was eight, years old.

Twice by his hateful, spiteful father, and another by a deranged matron. When he was placed in an orphanage for the second time.

Who was then exposed to death, and even more human suffering when he was 9. From having to bear the despair of lying in the arms of the only woman who befriended him. While she lied dying holding him in her arms.

Then when he was 12. Having to witness his only friend his own age. Being shoot before his eyes by his friends own father, with a shoot gun, and that's only what I personally leaned of while I held him in my arms as he trembled violently reliving the horrors hat transpired in his lifetime.

Like I said your father never knew what it was to be loved, or how to show affection. Who knew no way of showing concern any other way than by expressing himself sexually?

Your father was a person who live on the streets, and slept in woodsheds since he was 9. Who was forced to witness life at its worst?

One who had to have to learn how to survive by using people, and doing what he had to regardless of the consequences, or his feelings.

Even if it meant having to kill. Doing so at the age of 12. Who was sought more by the police than he was by his own family

He was a person who never belonged, or held anyone a bay from getting near to him. Who would rather stand alone, rather than to commit himself to anyone but, his one, and only benefactor.

Who believed that locality only lied in one's ability to use it against him. Only relying on himself and trusting in on one but, himself.

When I came into his life, and up until the day he died only trusted in me. Where he lived in dire fear.

Over what he had in me would be taken away, and he would be helplessly alone, and venerable because his inability to be able to function by himself, because of me taking him out of the only life he ever known.

Where he based his life on the so intent of him dying before me because he wasn't man enough to end his own life in the event that I died before him.

Where under it all your father was a man living in fear everyday of his life but, not willing to except that he was venerable to his worse fear as long as he still had me.

That's right honey. Regardless what you might have seen and heard. Underneath that hardcore exterior. There never was a more carrying, compassionate, and generous person than you father. Who hated himself for not being able to overcome his dependency on me not out living him.

Hate me if you most but, please wait before you judge me, and take the time now to mourn the loss of those who loved you with all their hearts.

Honey I can't stress strongly enough that not only this letter but my journal as well. Is for your eyes only.

That in the event if anything of what you will be discovering shouldn't fall into anyone of those hands who were involved with your father's activities should never happen.

As well as to why it's essential that the names that were mentioned in my journal have to be fictitious, as well as the state, or states connected to them including your father and I. In the event that this letter or my journal should fall into the wrong hand.

As well as how there would be no point in persecuting innocent people, or drawing unwarranted suspicions on who was, or where. Where you alone already know the answers to where you grew up.

Finding out the truth about your father, and what he did to make your life as satisfying, and rewarding as it was, and obviously still is best left forgotten.

Honey it wasn't my intent to turn you against him. I never wanted you to stop loving him with all your heart and soul but, things had to appear that way for all are sakes.

That's why I wrote in my journal about your father so that you will know the whole truth about the sort of man he was, and how much he really loved and cared for us both.

Reading what you already have reminds me of an old adage. "One can take the sailor out of the sea, but one can take the sea out of the sailor."

What Tom did was to him satisfying and rewarding to his family. It wasn't too him. As you have already read. Your father lived the life of a Nomad.

Who was befriend, them adopted, and nurtured by a figure head in a crime family. That's all he's even know how to be was a criminal.

I never thought it possible for anyone to live a double life, but yet we both did it, but your father took it further than that, and was doing it right under even my nose. Without me even being the wiser, and in doing so almost turned me into a criminal as well.

Making me out as no better than he was. While leaving me to live with the guilt of what I done. Not knowing that I wasn't doing it for me, but for him.

Which will torment me until my dying day. Knowing that I could never tell his daughter what I did to him out of fear that she would hate, and resent me for killing her father.

My revenge was also his other way he was going to make me suffer, like he suffered. Knowing that I killed someone who I love, and cherished with all my heart, and having to live with the guilt of living off the misery of so many others. Who made all those millions possible.

As they waited like vultures to get something on me.

Honey the fact that you're reading this letter is because I've passed on. I want you to know though I'm not there with you your father and I will always be close by, and that we are in a better place now,

Love forever and always.

* * * *

As it turned out during the years that followed I forgot about my mother's journal while perusing to finish high school.

Finally graduating from high school, and went off to college. Not giving any thought to asking or thinking about asking to read her journal.

Concentrating on completing my collage curriculum so that I could graduate in the top ten, of my class,

Where afterwards I opened my own business as a travel agency. Where I took advantage of the benefits I obtained from it. After building it up for over three years.

To retire early, and along with my inheritance I took myself a cruise overseas to visit Paris, Italy, and France, and did a bit of additional traveling to other counties. Visiting other ports of interest and opening a few more travel agencies before I returned back to the states.

That wasn't until I reached the age of forty-six, and finally I read my mother's journal. When I decided to tell my mother's story once and for all.

Seeing how she was out of the reach of the law, and was thinking of settling down with my husband and two children where at first I just started writing her story.

CHAPTER 15

My mother died at the age of thirty-nine the years was 1981. For seven more years I devoted to my life to my education and building a successful business. After which I sent a great deal of my life traveling overseas where I married, and had two children.

Before returning back to the United States at forty-six, where I stood with my husband, and two children in the cemetery before my mother's crypt speaking to my children and husband. Noticing a tall man, and woman a standing off in the distance by a tree at the top of a hill from my parent's crypt sight.

Looking somewhat familiar, but too far away for me to make out if I could recognize them clearly. Where their presence somewhat irritated me to the point where I was actually thinking about going up to confront them out of curiosity if nothing else but when I last looked up towards them they disappeared.

Leaving me with an eerie chilling feeling that I couldn't shake. Which caused me to continuous keep looking up in the direction where I spotted them.

Thinking back over everything about what my mother told me. Which I felt was practically everything before she died, and thinking that I leant the rest from her journal I was holding in my hand.

Which was in my estimation was the most incredible story I ever heard. Leaving out the most important facet of her story. That of whether she did, or didn't really murder my father.

I had my mother's remains placed in a crypt to be entombed along with my father's ashes that she bought back home with her, and had placed in the family crypt that she had built to include me as well.

Large enough that it would even have plenty of room for my husband as well as my children. If they wanted to be buried with me.

During my mother's illness my mother's mother Donna took care of me until I went off to college.

DISPLACEMENT INTENT

Where my mother's brothers lived pretty much on their own while growing up themselves, and starting families of their own but, they always made it a point to come visit their sister along with their mother on a regular basis while I was gone.

The house my mother bought was a rather large house. That needed to have a caretaker Who lived in the caretaker's house so he could be around to maintain the grounds, and make repairs to the property whenever needed.

While vacationing in Italy before my mother's passed my mother also bought a place somewhat larger than the one she had back in the states, and up until her passing she made it a point to take Art. Leaving Donna to heir a temporary caretaker until she came back to pick up living her life even during while she was having to deal with her cancer.

Becoming so dependent on Art that she would take him every time she would go overseas to visit her other place, and bring him back with her when she came back home to continue her treatments.

Too manage any work that needed to be done to the new place to keep the place in good condition while she was going to be living there. Then have him do it again when she came back home.

Having Art also hire qualified caretakers to maintain the place when she needed Art back home in the states to maintain her home there.

Every summer when school let out Art the caretaker and I would go overseas together to check on my mother's place.

Where we would spend the entire summer touring different places like Paris, Rome, and England.

Before returning back home to the states to be there for my mother, and to pick up my life with my friends, and returning back to school

Art sort of became a father figure to me. I always thought of him as more than a caretaker. That's how close the three of us became to each other. I guess that he just grew on me to a point where I came to rely on him for everything as well as my mother until she past.

Giving him a room of his own in the main house so that he would be near her. Seeing how he was always at her side to be there to take care of her during her illness.

My mother gave Art a permanent home in her will next to the main house she purchased overseas, and saw to it that he had a lifetime job taking care of the place in Italy for as long as he wanted it.

After she died Art and I continued to go overseas. The next summer while going to check out now my place overseas was doing.

Art met, and fell in love with a wonderful woman by the name of Patty. Where the three of us sort of hit it off and sort of became family together.

Where I have to admit it that I was the one who sort of manipulated Art into marrying her. Uncanny as it seemed Patty reminded me a great deal of my mother in so many ways. I guess that's why I instantly became so smitten by her.

Where that's why Art became so smitten by her as well, and they had so much in common with each of us. It was as if we were meant to be together that's now much we all bonded together.

From the time Art first met her it only took less than maybe a few days before I was referring to her as (Mother) and as for Art it was darling, or honey with her. Referring back to him the same way and me as dear, or sweetheart.

After they married I virtually had to force them to return with me back to the states. Where I wanted them to live into the main house. Seeing how only Donna, my mothers, mother was only going to be still living there with me

To live along with Donna and I, but they preferred to live in the caretaker's house, because two of my mother's brother were still living off and on in the main house.

Where they didn't want to be an imposition, by disrupting the family routine, but yet still be close by if they were needed for anything.

It didn't take much to figure out that it was their polite way of saying that they rather be alone. By the way the two of them were acting between themselves I would have to be totally blind not to see why.

Though they were both getting on in years it obviously didn't show by the way they were acting like teenagers literally infatuated with each other.

So I took it upon myself to have the caretakers house enlarged. Just in case they wanted to start a family. Even though they were getting on in years.

Patty, Donna, and I got along marvelously, While Art was still hitting it off

DISPLACEMENT INTENT

great with my brothers. As we all went along with establishing futures, and relationships for ourselves.

Where I eventually talked Art, and Patty into moving into the main convincing them into taking my mother's room.

So that I could lease the caretaker house to the new assistant caretaker. For services rendered accountable only to Art when he was in the states taking care of the property.

So the assistant caretaker could have a place to live when Art, Patty and I would go back overseas to live for the summer.

Until I graduated from high school. When we all went to live permanently overseas while I went to college.

The home in the states was more, or less given to Donna to live in as Art, Patty, and I lived overseas. Where I pursued opening another traveling agency, and found the love of my life.

Where I eventually found myself visiting Art, and Patty after moving out of my mother's place and into my new home to live with my husband to start a family of our own. As Art, and Patty went about living a comfortable rewarding life traveling, and taking ocean voltages enjoying their later years.

Art never told me was that Patty was a very rich woman herself. As for Art He had the house my mother gave him, and was investing the salary I was giving him. Seeing how he never had to spend any of it on himself where I was paying for everything.

Accumulating enough to where he really didn't need to continue to be my caretaker but, he loved what he was doing, and it gave them both an opportunity to spend time with me. So the matter of them ever wanting to leave me never came up.

Where I myself invested a great deal of time and effort in building up my traveling agency business because I loved doing what I was doing. While having myself two, wonderful children. Before I decided to return back to the states to continue living my life still continuing to visit Art, and Patty overseas.

With them promising me that nothing could ever stop them from coming to visit me, and my family.

As you can see my mother's story did in fact turn out to be my story. One that was filled with a lot of hardship, and despair for my parents, but one that actually did turn out for the best for everyone.

Though there's no way I could find out if everything my mother left me in her journal was in fact true.

If I could only believe some of what was written where I have no way to know if in fact my real father did die from what my mother did to him.

As will as if in fact she did what she said and decided to go for the millions, and to devote the rest of her live to my happiness

However, I personally know for certain that my mother did die from cancer. Even though I wasn't able to spend time with her while she was going through her treatments, and knowing that Art would have told me if I ask him seeing how he was the one spending most of the time with her.

If he wouldn't have then seeing how I was so young at the time. He would have assuredly told me while I was growing up and we were spending so much time together mostly just talking about her and how wonderful she was.

Even though Art wasn't one for sharing how hurt he felt when she past He did open himself up to me and told me how much he truly loved my mother where he never once said it to anyone else with the exception of Patty.

Where when I was with my mother she was always wanting me to concentrated on getting an education, and making a life for myself. In the event she wasn't around to do it for me.

Art never let up with bringing up the fact that I shouldn't let my mother down by not getting myself an education like she wanted for me to do.

What I always found strange was the way Art came into my mother's life, and the way my mother took to him right off. Even after a few relationships with men I really never got to become acquainted with all that much.

However, where Art was concern my mother couldn't wait for me to get to like him and was always asking my opinion about what I thought about him.

The more I thought about Art and those other guys. The only thing I thought that they had in common was they all appeared to have the same eyes.

Not only the color but also the shape where the face was totally different between each and every one of them. But that was so long ago and I'm a lot older now... But, I just don't know... Why it was those eyes that I keep thinking about...?

After reading my mother's journal she left a lot of doubt in my mind regarding my father's death as well as her passing, and her wanting to be cremated just like my father.

Then there was the large crypt she had built to have them both placed in but my mother was always a bit eccentric when it came to doing things her way.

I knew what my mother was going through, and that her pain and suffering was real. I spent time going along with her to the hospital, and even spoke to her doctors concerning her condition. Where all I ever got from him was. "It's best that your mother tells you because of your age."

I have pictures of her before she came down with cancer, and I've pictures of her deteriorating until her eventual death. I could never forget what she looked like even though I have seemed to have misplace a lot of those pictures over the years.

I also knew that there was no way there could be anyone but, her lying in rest in her crypt but, over the year's certain doubts that not even after reading her journal didn't answer but only compounded them even more.

Where I have to admit I can barely remember what my father looked like. Seeing how young I was at the time, and that I was finding myself glade that he died. No long having to be there witnessing what he was putting my mother through before he died.

It was troubling time for the entire family fir sure before his death even afterward in fact. During which I really didn't get to spend very much time with either of my parent, but that doesn't mean that I didn't love them both with all my heart in my own way, and wasn't hurt deeply when they died.

What I still do to this day find somewhat peculiar, if not uncanny is Patties mannerisms, and how they were so much like my mothers.

Where instead mimicking her mannerisms she also had extinguishing features that closely resemble my mother's but her overall appearance was totally different from when I last picture before she came down with cancer, and she changed so drastically during her illness.

Over the years my mother and father kept popping in and out of my mind with so much uncertainty associated with them when I took time to concentrate and really looking at Art, and Patty together.

Even them nothing like I last remembered seeing my parents together, and visualizing all the distortions that disrupted their appearance. That was nothing like what I was seeing when Art and Patty were together.

Even though Art himself was a very incredible man. He still was nothing more than a caretaker, and the way my mother took to him.

Where they came so close together didn't seem quite normal but, then again what did seem normal to a young very impressionable girl who was already emotionally distraught over the loss of her father.

Where the more Art was around the more I suppress any doubts, or concerns I might of had about him but even now those eyes of his still haunt me, but yet they seem so familiar but yet so very distant…

You might be asking why I want to pursue publishing my mother's story. Well to be totally honest with you, as well as myself.

It's all I have, along with a few pictures of my parents, and no very clear ones of my father. That I could have for my kids to remember them by.

Then I can't stop from wondering. What if my father really didn't die but, not only pulling off the prefect crime but, whether or not if they actually pulled it off?

Convincing even the syndicate as well. Actually absconding with as much as my mother was to be believed she was actually worth.

'What do you think…?'

I found myself asking myself when I came to stand before the close door of my parent's crypt. Along with my husband and two children.

When I first came back home after spending so many years away. Holding the letter in my hand that I accidentally dropped. That I just finished reading to myself.

It was because of that letter, and what my mother said in it that prompted me to write their story from out of curiosity hoping to find the answer.

DISPLACEMENT INTENT

To what I was to be able to understand and still wasn't able to put an ending to her story that she felt sure that I would. Feeling that I let her down.

Wondering what I would have done if I was in her position. As I stood saliently reading my mother's last word in silence to myself. It read:

My dearest Sally in my safe in the bedroom you'll find another white envelope with your father's name on it. After you read what's inside you'll know what to do.

Though my life is now over. It's just now beginning. What's said inside is for your eyes only. You mustn't tell anyone about what I stated to you in the journal, or any of the letters that I left for you. It's that crucial to your future. I'm sorry that I can't be there with you but, I'll always be here by for as long as you need me to be

By now you're obviously grown and natured to where you can live your own life without your father and me as I knew you would make me extremely proud of you. We both loved you with all are hearts never forget that.

Honey your father and I are both very sorry that we had to deceive you, but it was the only way to insure that we would have a life together, and give you the life you so richly deserve.

The futures that have established where done so purposely for you to be able to share openly without having to worry about your future where ours was never meant to be.

You know the whole story but, not the rest of the story. That my dear I think you've pretty much figured out already even if you are still harboring doubts.

If you figured it out right. You'll also know the answer to the question you are must likely asking yourself about your father and me, and our love for you.

This letter is with love from your Mother, and too your family, and to say. You did your father and I very proud.

I know now that I left you in good hands when I had to leave but, if it's any consolation I never as well as your father never stopped looking out for you."

"Honey what does this letter mean?" Harry looked over my shoulder reading the letter along with me asking.

"It's a long story dear." I replied. You know I think we'll take the kids this year's when we go back overseas to visit our very old and dear friends that we left to come here so that our children could get to know my parent's relatives. Before they too miss out on not knowing them a lot better like I did you parents and relatives.

I'm sure the kids will just love living here with them as you well. Seeing how they're already family to all of us.

If it wasn't for the fact that I know for sure that here was where my parents first met and this is where they would want to be I would move their crypt back overseas so that we could all live and die together along with your family.

Where that's not possible with my mother's family being here where I know leaving my parents here is where I know they would want to be but.

Regretful knowing that their life stopped here. Where ours began somewhere else that's going to eventually separate all of us from each other.

Having to realize that once my mothers, mother and brothers pass on I'm going to be all that remains that's going to remember my parents by. That I wasn't his son to carry on his name like your son is going to do for you.

I would really like to know the truth. Not just what Patty and Art supposedly think they know about my parents. After reading from my mother's journal it's clear that they knew nothing at all about what my parents were really like.

Art only knew my mother and me and I really didn't know all that much about what really went on between my parents.

As for Patty she could only know what Art obviously must have told her about what my mother told him about my father, and all I've to rely on with what my mother wrote about to me.

I think that I'm going to take some time to write the story that will tell all about my family history. Just in case our children might want to read about them some day.

After all it is their family history… Even though it's going to stop with me and begins with yours. I never had myself a brother."

"Honey are you ever going to let me read that journal your mother left you?"

"Nope, she said it was for my eyes only. I guess that you will just have to wait until I leave it in my will or maybe buy the book if I get it published.

If and where you do. I want you to do me a favor. Leave it for our children to read it, and not to hesitate to give their opinion on what they really think about my father, and whether my mother did, or didn't. As for me I personally believe that I finally figured it out."

THE END

www.ingramcontent.com/pod-product-compliance
Lightning Source LLC
Chambersburg PA
CBHW071430070526
44578CB00001B/64